YORK NOTES

General Editors: Professor A.N. Jeffares (*University of Stirling*) & Professor Suheil Bushrui (*American University of Beirut*)

This book is due for return on or before the last date shown below.

WITHDRAWN

S

YORK PRESS
Immeuble Esseily, Place Riad Solh, Beirut.

LONGMAN GROUP UK LIMITED
Longman House, Burnt Mill, Harlow,
Essex CM20 2JE, England
and Associated Companies throughout the World.

First published 1982
Reprinted 1989

ISBN 0-582-78209-0

Produced by Longman Group (FE) Ltd
Printed in Hong Kong

Contents

Part 1

Introduction

THOMAS HARDY WAS BORN IN DORSET, in the south of England, in 1840. Nearly all his novels are set in the south-western area of England that he called Wessex, of which Dorset is a part. The Wessex he describes in his later novels is 'a modern Wessex of railways, the penny post, mowing and reaping machines, union workhouses, lucifer matches, labourers who could read and write, and National school children'. (Preface to his novel *Far from the Madding Crowd*, 1895). The Wessex he describes in *The Woodlanders*, however, is a country of woods and orchards where people live by hollow-turning, barking, spar-making, hurdle-making, tree-planting, felling and cider-making. Rural Wessex is slow and old-fashioned. It is as though time has stopped. There is something dreamlike and haunting about daily activities. The people themselves seem to be dwarfed by the vegetation; life is primitive.

As a boy his long walks to school brought him close to the country and its customs. One of his family's favourite walks was to Rainbarrow where Hardy's father would look through a telescope at the surrounding country. Hardy himself loved to look at things from a distance or a height, as he does in *The Woodlanders*. His father introduced him to the business world of the stone-mason, and to nature; his mother introduced him to history and legend. Family and local history interested him much more than what went on in the world at large. His parents sometimes told him stories of violence which haunted him because he had a sensitive, morbid nature. (On one occasion he watched with interest the public hanging of a woman.) His curiosity was abnormal. He loved animals and small creatures which seemed to him to have a timelessness that man did not. A good example in *The Woodlanders* is Grace's observation of the small creatures of the woods in Chapter 41.

Hardy hated physical contact. As a boy he was precocious, enjoying older company, and loved playing the fiddle. He was quietly-spoken, well-read, and ambitious. Of himself Hardy said that 'a clue to much of his character and action throughout his life is afforded by his lateness of development in virility'.* He was always reticent about his sexual life. Who is to blame him?

At sixteen he was apprenticed to an architect and spent all his spare time on study. When he moved to London the young country boy was

*F. E. Hardy: *Life of Thomas Hardy*, London, 1962, *Volume 1*, p. 32.

shocked by office conversations and by open prostitution in Cremorne Gardens. But London was the right place for him to enjoy the music he loved so much and to acquire more knowledge. He appears to have been a keen collector of information. Hardy grew bored by his architectural training because it was too mechanical and because, being a young man from the country, he did not have the social contacts necessary to enable him to gain contracts from the wealthy. After a year in London he decided to return to literature and his own education; architecture became a secondary interest. His first love was poetry which he wrote throughout his life, and he was determined also to master the craft of writing fiction.

In 1867 he returned to Dorset for health reasons as an architect's assistant. Here he wrote the draft of his first novel *The Poor Man and the Lady*. Macmillan the publisher rejected it and Hardy later destroyed it. He remained determined to succeed as a writer. *Desperate Remedies* was his first novel to be published. It was an edition of five hundred copies and Hardy had to pay seventy-five pounds towards the cost. Reviews were mixed but at least he was praised for his ability to describe nature and create authentic local atmosphere. Hardy, who was continuing his work restoring churches, was desperately short of money. Then he was invited to publish *A Pair of Blue Eyes* in monthly parts in *Tinsley's Magazine*. He was glad to accept, and it proved to be good practice for him in mastering the art of serial writing.

Leslie Stephen, editor of *The Cornhill Magazine*, volunteered in 1872 to publish his next novel which was to be *Far from the Madding Crowd*. While Hardy was at work on the novel his friend and tutor, Moule, killed himself. From now on his heroes and heroines become tragic figures. In 1874 he married Emma Gifford. His intellect attracted her; her vitality attracted him. Their first home was at Sturminster where he wrote *The Return of the Native* which was his best novel so far. Today it remains one of his most popular, despite its intense gloom.

Later novels well worth reading are *The Mayor of Casterbridge* (1886), *Tess of the D'Urbervilles* (1891), and *Jude the Obscure* (1896).

While working on *The Mayor of Casterbridge* he agreed to write a 'woodland story' in serial form for *Macmillan's Magazine*. This was to become *The Woodlanders*, which Hardy classified as one of his 'Novels of Character and Environment'. Because *Jude the Obscure* caused such a public outcry Hardy decided to write no more novels. He devoted the rest of his life to writing poetry. Although his marriage with Emma Gifford had not been particularly happy, when she died he wrote one of the finest series of love poems in the English language. The year the First World War broke out he married again and worked on his collections of verse until he died in 1928. His ashes were buried in Westminster Abbey (and his heart in Stinson churchyard).

Hardy wrote regional novels – narratives confined to a district. Britain is a small island. Its inhabitants are insular in outlook. It is natural for writers to choose local settings because they know them and because they think they are important. The regional or country novel was common in England in the nineteenth century, and the outlook of the English novelist is narrow compared with that of, say, the Russian, who takes a broad view. Some people still thought that God made the country and man made the town. Hardy, who was a member of the Anglican Church and who attended services mainly to hear the music, did not believe that God made the country. After looking for God for fifty years, Hardy thought that if he had existed he would have discovered him by then.

Hardy did not think that to confine his novels to Wessex was to limit them in any way. What happens in Wessex is what happens elsewhere. The tensions, conflicts, and dilemmas that people experience here are common to mankind, and he believed that what happened to people in a local district could be presented in such a way as to have universal application and appeal.

There was a tradition of country writing behind him. For example there is Jane Austen's *Emma* in which polite people talk to one another and arrange marriages in country houses; there is Elizabeth Gaskell's *Cranford* in which old ladies take tea and discuss matters of etiquette; there are Trollope's novels about church affairs in Barsetshire; there is George Eliot's *Silas Marner* about town and country. Perhaps the best known regional novelist after Hardy is D. H. Lawrence, who in *The Rainbow* (1915) and *Women in Love* (1921) explores male-female relationships and society on the borders of Nottinghamshire and Derbyshire.

Hardy does not, of course, choose to describe the country of Wessex just for the sake of the description. He does it so that we can see men and women living in a landscape that is timeless and unchangeable. His Wessex is a district full of history, legend, and folklore. It has its own local customs such as bonfires and May festivities, its own superstitions about Midsummer eve, and its own quaint habits of speech. Wessex is a character itself.

Because Hardy's world occupies such a small area, the characters live near one another and frequently meet one another. That accounts for some of the complaints about coincidence in Hardy's novels. It is inevitable that his characters bump into one another. They don't meet by chance; they just cannot help meeting. Hardy said that by limiting the action of the novel to Wessex he created a 'unity of place . . . seldom preserved in novels', and he provided his readers with a map of the area. At the back of his mind were the Greek tragedies of Aeschylus (525–456BC) and Sophocles (496–406BC).

In *The Woodlanders* (Chapter 1), Hardy suggests that we are about to experience tragedy of a high order:

It was one of those sequestered spots outside the gates of the world where may usually be found more meditation than action, and more listlessness than meditation; where reasoning proceeds on narrow premisses, and results in inferences wildly imaginative; yet where, from time to time, dramas of a grandeur and unity truly Sophoclean are enacted in the real, by virtue of the concentrated passions and closely-knit interdependence of the lives therein.

But there is no character in the novel of the stature of a tragic protagonist. Grace Melbury, the most complex character in the novel, does not reach such dramatic heights.

In writing the novel Hardy was not setting out to prove anything. He believed that a novel should not argue a case for or against something. Instead it should be an impression – a writer's impression of life. Hardy's impression in *The Woodlanders* is that well-meaning parents cause chaos; that education blights natural impulses and confuses relationships between men and women; that country characters will survive doing what they have been doing for centuries; that Nature is cruel, and that nothing will change.

Hardy believed that no story was worth writing unless it were exceptional or unusual. A reader is not interested in the dreary description of everyday commonplace events however real or true they may be. He believed that the novelist should satisfy the reader's 'love of the uncommon in human experience'. He also thought that the writer had to strike a balance between the portrayal of ordinary life and the portrayal of a life that is extraordinary. If the novelist did not do this, his story would be unreal, unconvincing, too strange. The characters themselves must be convincing. They cannot be abnormal because the reader has to recognise them as part of human nature; as people in whom he believes. The unusual in fiction, then, must be in the events and not the characters. A lover dying in a storm within yards of his beloved and security, the superstitious sowing at a Midsummer eve ritual, the setting of a trap to maim a man, the felling of a tree that shocks and kills a man – these are not common events.

In England, as in Russia, the novel became the most widely-read form of literature in the nineteenth century because it was the best means of portraying the life of the middle classes who had acquired money and power and who had leisure to read. Lending libraries flourished and magazines which included serials were popular. The novelist knew his reader and knew what he wanted to read because he shared his views on religion, love, status, ambition, marital status, and fortune. He also had a similar background to his reader.

Novels were mainly written by middle-class people for middle-class people who wanted to see themselves, people they recognised, a society they knew, values they upheld reflected in their reading. People wanted to read about themselves in novels in the nineteenth century just as people in the twentieth century want to see themselves in family comedies and other programmes about ordinary life on television. They wanted to be entertained by what they felt rang true.

The social history of England in the nineteenth century is in the novels. Take a sample of novels published in one decade and you will find that they highlight the values of English society: Dickens, *The Mystery of Edwin Drood*, 1870; George Eliot, *Middlemarch*, 1871-2; Trollope, *The Way We Live Now*, 1875; Hardy, *The Return of the Native*, 1878; Meredith, *The Egoist*, 1879.

During this period the more powerful and newly-rich middle classes of the Whig party, were competing with the old aristocracy (Tories) for power. In English fiction the old nobility are often presented as eccentrics, sources of amusement, pompous asses, gluttons, lecherous old men and flirtatious old women. Invariably they are comic figures because the novelists are Whigs whose point of view we are invited to adopt. It is also true, of course, that much of the old aristocracy was stupid and gross, and sat on its inherited land in complacent unawareness of the poverty around it and of the hardships it imposed.

Hardy is more interested in human aspirations and relationships than he is in social criticism. Love, marriage, and the family are central in his novels. He was also the first English novelist to explore male-female relationships outside marriage. This caused scandal in a Victorian society which pretended in public that sex did not exist and which acted in private as it saw fit. *Tess of the D'Urbervilles* (1891) and *Jude the Obscure* (1896), in particular, aroused public indignation.

A note on the text

Hardy started writing *The Woodlanders* at his house in Dorchester, Dorset, in November 1885. The work was to appear in serial form in twelve monthly parts for *Macmillan's Magazine* from 1886 to 1887. As each episode was published he went on to write the next. The story was also published in serial form in the American magazine *Harper's Bazaar*. Hardy invited the publisher to choose from the two titles he submitted – either *The Woodlanders* or *Fitzpiers at Hintock*; Macmillan published the former, in three volumes, in 1887. Hardy's preface and postscript appeared together for the first time in the 1912 Wessex edition. Hardy revised the text frequently. In a note in The New Wessex Edition of *The Woodlanders* (Macmillan, London, 1974), David Lodge points out that there are eight slightly different versions.

Part 2

Summaries
of THE WOODLANDERS

A general summary

The woodlands are dense and extensive. In autumn the fallen leaves completely cover the track of the old coachroad. The setting is lonely: a stranger appears on the scene, lost. Mrs Dollery's horse knows every inch of the road between Abbot's Cernel and Sherton. The women in the back of the cart describe Barber Percomb, the stranger, as being too proud and snobbish to have a hairdresser's sign outside his shop. He thinks he is superior to other hairdressers.

Hardy introduces Little Hintock as a peaceful retreat cut off from the world. Little ever happens. As Percomb leaves the cart on his strange errand, one of the women tells him of a new young doctor who is in league with the devil and practises medicine in the village. Both Percomb and the doctor strike an ominous note which is strengthened by Hardy's warning that sometimes 'dramas of grandeur and unity truly Sophoclean are enacted in the real, by virtue of the concentrated passions and closely-knit interdependence of the lives' of people in places like Little Hintock.

Through a door he observes Marty South hard at work. She is about twenty and has beautiful hair, which Percomb wants to buy for a Mrs Charmond who is going overseas again. Refusing his offer, she tends her ailing father, before going out to work in Melbury's timber yard, where she overhears Melbury telling his wife that he wants his daughter Grace to marry Giles Winterborne – the man of whom Marty is fond. She cuts off her hair in despair. With the rape of her locks Marty feels that she has been seduced by the devil.

Morning comes. Creatures of the night withdraw, as the woodlanders start their copse-work. There is a feeling that the tradition of spar-making, sawing, and crib-framing will be long-lived because they are part of the natural order of things in the woods. The woodlanders describe Mrs Charmond as a woman of loose behaviour, Grace as an over-educated young lady, Fitzpiers as a strange young man who reads. They gossip as they work.

On his way to meet Grace at Sherton Abbas, Giles meets Marty on her way to the barber's with the locks that will later lure Fitzpiers. The meeting of Grace in her finery and Giles with his apple tree is awkward. Mrs Charmond gives Marty a lift home. Giles finds that Grace has changed; she cannot identify an apple. She is glad to talk of places she has been, provided she does not have to speak about herself. 'She had fallen from the good old Hintock ways.' After her return home she is attracted to a light at the doctor's house, and after a conversation with Grammer Oliver, she goes to bed thinking of a doctor destined for higher things.

The next day Giles follows Melbury and his daughter to an auction where, fascinated by flakes of snow falling on Grace's hair, he buys wood he does not need, and later apologises to Melbury for bidding against him. He finds the Melbury household more interested in preparing Grace for a visit to the House than in himself. Grace is drawn to two people who come from the outside world – Mrs Charmond and Dr Fitzpiers.

Giles watches her going eagerly to the House, where Grace is fascinated by a collection of man-traps and by the conversation of a sophisticated woman who has travelled. The scene shifts to the tree-planting, shared by Marty and Giles who 'had a marvellous power of making trees grow'. Marty hears the trees sighing when planted 'because they are very sorry to begin life in earnest – just as we be'. Giles watches Grace returning from the House; Fitzpiers watches her through an eyeglass behind a hedge; Giles watches Fitzpiers.

Giles feels insignificant because of the way Grace talks about books over his head, and thinks that she is still a true-hearted girl because of her love for Hintock. He decides on a Christmas party to bring things to a head. The Melbury family arrives too early; Giles is embarrassed – the fates are against him – and furniture oil stains Grace's dress. Creedle accidentally splashes stew on her face. Grace, having forgotten the old dances, and thinking of new ones she enjoyed in a large house elsewhere, does not join in. She is an outsider. Her father knows she does not belong with the woodlanders. When Giles hears that there was a slug on her plate, he concludes that he has no chance of winning her now.

Mrs Melbury thinks that Grace will marry Giles 'as an understood thing'; Grace thinks she should marry him as a point of honour; Melbury, who has vowed over the grave of Giles's father that Grace will marry Giles, fears that her education will be wasted and that she will adopt the manners and habits of the locals. The rudeness of a hunter to Grace confirms his belief that she should marry a gentleman, and not somebody who looks like himself. Grace is unhappy because she is not ready yet to devote her life to Giles, because she feels like property in which her father has invested. The tone of this section of the novel is ominous: Mrs Charmond, with her new hair, leaves for overseas the next day without Grace; the property of Giles Winterborne becomes Mrs Charmond's if John South dies; Grace breaks off her engagement to Giles who stays up the elm tree he is pruning instead of pursuing her; on the doctor's advice two woodmen cut the tree down, the shock of which kills South.

Giles gives Grace the horse he bought. Melbury points out kindly but firmly that he cannot marry Grace because he no longer has a house. Marty, feeling sorry for Giles, writes on the wall outside his house:

'O Giles! you've lost your dwelling place,
And therefore, Giles, you'll lose your Grace.'

After reading this, Giles writes a formal letter to Melbury breaking the engagement. The next morning, thinking that Giles will see her, Grace rubs out 'lose' and puts in 'keep'. She is warming to Giles and tells her father she wants the engagement to continue. He shows her the letter. Too late. She did not know if he had seen her writing on the wall. It is a situation that Hardy loves. If only . . . 'Fate, it seemed, would have it this way, and there was nothing to do but to acquiesce.' Giles, who did not see her, retires from the scene of human action. Her gesture of love is lost forever.

Edred Fitzpiers, handsome and sharp-eyed, watches from his window as Suke Damson, then Marty South, open the newly-painted swing-gate. A third woman approaches. 'She walked as delicately as if she had been bred in town, and as firmly as if she had been bred in the country.' He is attracted because there is no crude rusticity about this one. She fills a need, perhaps temporary, within himself. There is a marked contrast between the pretentious conversation of Fitzpiers and the natural talk of Giles to whom the doctor admits: '. . . I am in love with something in my own head, and no thing-in-itself outside it at all.' The woman Fitzpiers sees then is not so much Grace as an extension of his imagination. Alone and isolated, with no interest in Hintock or its history, the doctor creates an ideal mistress out of his head and allows her to take the form of Grace, with whom he intends a casual relationship or a flirtation. She will relieve the monotony of his life.

After spending time with the men barking the trees and hearing old stories of the woods and supernatural agents, Fitzpiers wonders if he could settle down here in 'quiet domesticity' and 'calm contentment'. He tells Grace that he would like to propose marriage if she were ready for such a proposal. Grace, unable to make up her mind, tells him she still likes Giles. They stand in an awkward silence. Two birds quarrelling in a branch above them fall into the hot ashes at their feet and singe themselves. If Fitzpiers and Grace settle down as husband and wife, if they clip their wings, they too are going to hurt themselves.

On Midsummer eve when the local girls are creating a spell to reveal their future partners, Grammer Oliver predicts the marriage of Grace and the doctor. She thinks that he should marry Mrs Charmond and that Grace should marry Giles Winterborne. Fitzpiers has no sooner embraced Grace than he is in pursuit of the provocative Suke Damson lying in wait in a hay-cock. They spend the night together. The other girls run away, frightened by the appearance of a short, fat man in evening dress who comes from South Carolina, and who is seeking Mrs Charmond. Later he is to be the death of her.

Grace finds Fitzpiers exciting, intoxicating. It is not love or ambition but 'a fearful consciousness of hazard in the air'. There is something melancholy and romantic about his family's history. Grace, who has never thought of marrying him, now hears Fitzpiers declare that they will marry in a registry office so that none of his future patients in Budmouth will know anything of his wife's past. He is selfish, snobbish, and a liar. He tells Grace that Suke Damson came to his house early in the morning to have a tooth out. She believes him and agrees to marry him in a church. Giles Winterborne has withdrawn into himself until the cider-making season comes around.

Hard at work, he is watched by Grace from the Earl of Wessex inn. It would have been too hard a life for her. Her father was right, she thinks, and she feels superior to Giles. After all it was the finger of Fate that controlled their destinies. Fitzpiers despises the woodlanders and is apprehensive about returning home after the honeymoon. His attitude disappoints Grace. Ironically Fitzpiers discovers that he has lost the respect of the local people in marrying one of them. Married for two months, he now sees what it meant to choose Grace instead of a career.

The doctor calls on Mrs Charmond after her accident. To him she is languid, poised, sophisticated, and romantic. They attach great importance to the fact that they met and kissed at Heidelberg when he was a student. They talk like lovers about their embryonic passion. 'But see how powerless is the human will against predestination. We were prevented meeting; we have met.' The dialogue is melodramatic. Fitzpiers refuses the practice at Budmouth so that he can be near the woman or enchantress who exerts such a power over him. If Giles had been allowed to keep his house he could have married Grace, and she could have had Fitzpiers. Mrs Charmond has to laugh at the irony of fate.

When Grace discovers that her husband is calling on Mrs Charmond at Middleton Abbey, she is not greatly excited or jealous. Autumn's abundance surrounds Fitzpiers as he rides into the distance with a deep violet sky behind him. The faithless Fitzpiers is on Darling, the horse the faithful Giles gave Grace. Just as Grace sees him disappear from sight, Giles appears with his cider equipment.

'He looked and smelt like Autumn's very brother, his face being sunburnt to wheat-colour, his eyes blue as corn-flowers, his sleeves and leggings dyed with fruit-stains, his hands clammy with the sweet juice of apples . . .' It is a sensuous description conveying the vitality and naturalness of Giles. This is a powerful moment for Grace – almost like a divine revelation.

Her heart rose from its late sadness like a released bough; her senses revelled in the sudden lapse back to Nature unadorned. The consciousness of having to be genteel because of her husband's profession, the veneer of artificiality which she had acquired at the fashionable schools, were thrown off, and she became the crude country girl of her latent early instincts.

And then she learns that Suke Damson has all her teeth. Her husband is a liar. To please her father she has degraded herself. The marriage was a mistake. She now respects in Giles the homeliness, the country dress, and the roughness, and wishes she had never gone to fashionable schools. 'I hate genteel life.' Her father, on hearing that she wished she were like Marty South, tells Giles that Grace still loves him, and interferes again by appealing to Mrs Charmond to let Fitzpiers go.

Unhinged and agitated by Melbury's appeal and by the distress she has caused his daughter, Mrs Charmond goes for a walk in the woods she hates, meets Grace, and confesses all. She says she loves Fitzpiers but will do her best not to see him. Lost in the woods, the two women spend the night together, and are reconciled to one another. Mrs Charmond writes to Fitzpiers begging him not to see her again. She is going to Europe. Grace is not well and stays with an acquaintance for a while. Fitzpiers, whose medical practice is deteriorating rapidly, receives from Marty a letter disclosing the source of his mistress's hair. It is not opened. Melbury, whose intention was to plead with Fitzpiers, now decides to give him a piece of his mind as he follows him from Hintock House on the wrong horse.

Fitzpiers, thrown from his horse, and fortified with rum on an empty stomach, reveals his hatred of Hintock; complains that he is not appreciated; confesses his love for Mrs Charmond; and admits that he would enjoy being a free man if anything were to happen to Grace, who is already ill. Melbury throws him from the horse. Fitzpiers picks himself up and wanders off into the woods. Grace is no sooner home than Suke Damson, closely followed by Felice Charmond, arrive distressed and concerned about Fitzpiers. 'You shall know all I know. Indeed, you have a perfect right to go into his bedroom; who can have a better than either of you?' The sharpness of her remark is lost on the tearful women who do not see themselves as victims of the doctor's selfishness. Grace sees how attractive he is: 'There was, in truth, a lovebird yearning to fly from her heart; and it wanted a lodging badly.'

Fitzpiers, recalled to life and health with Mrs Charmond's assistance, writes a farewell letter to Grace declaring that he cannot live in the Melbury house after her father's treatment of him. Grace's health declines. Fitzpiers, then Felice Charmond, leave for Europe. Melbury, persuaded that his daughter will be a free woman soon because of a new divorce law, sends her a letter of reassurance from London. Giles remains sceptical about the alleged new law. Grace and Giles meet at the Sherton market, confess their love, and decide to wait for things to be settled. Even here the conflict in Grace is highlighted when she feels humiliated by having to eat in a simple old inn. It offends the 'superficial and transitory taste' of one used to dining in style at the Earl of Wessex.

There is no hope of a speedy divorce. Giles is ill in a hut. 'A feverish indisposition which had been hanging about him for some time, the result of a chill caught the previous winter, seemed to acquire virulence with the prostration of his hopes.' Grace flees from the house on learning that Fitzpiers is coming, and asks Giles to accompany her to a friend's house. It is raining heavily. He offers her his hut. Because of honour and propriety, he stays outside. As the rain penetrates his primitive shelter, Giles feels weak and ill. Stoical pride supports him. Fifty yards from Grace he lies dying. Summer has gone and the autumn rain has set in. A storm develops. Grace behaves as she does because of the vow she made to another man. Yet she does make the grand gesture. Giles refuses her invitation to come into the hut. A day passes and she finds him raving, delirious. Dr Fitzpiers is summoned. Too late: Giles dies. The wood is a house of death. The trees seem to miss him – especially the young trees which he had planted and which 'were at that very moment sending out their roots in the direction that he had given them with his subtle hand'.

Fitzpiers quarrelled with Mrs Charmond and teased her about her false hair. After he left, the disappointed gentleman from South Carolina killed her. What Fitzpiers now wants is forgiveness. Grace made him think that she had slept with Giles. Now he learns from Marty the truth and sends Grace a love letter. They meet but her heart is not in it because it is in the grave with Giles. At night Fitzpiers haunts Grace's house. Tim Tangs watches him. He resents Suke's interest in the doctor. He knows that his marriage is a failure. New Zealand will repair no damage. Bent on vengeance, he sets a man-trap to maim Fitzpiers.

When he finds his wife's dress in the trap, Fitzpiers is grief-stricken. His cries come from the heart. Grace hears him: they embrace, and are reconciled. She promises to come with him to his new practice in the Midlands. Melbury has little faith in the reconciliation, believing that 'the woman walks and laughs somewhere at this very moment whose neck he'll be coling next year as he does hers to-night; and as he did Felice Charmond's last year; and Suke Damson's the year afore!' The woodlanders joke about the absurdities of love and marriage. *The Woodlanders* ends with the pathetic Marty grieving over Giles and glad that she now has him all to herself.

Detailed summaries

Chapter 1

Mrs Dollery's cart brings the women home from market. The hairdresser Percomb hitches a ride.

NOTES AND GLOSSARY:

title-page:	in these lines of verse Hardy means that the most enchanting bedroom or cottage cannot protect an ill-matched couple from the buffets of life
dumpy level:	a spirit level with a squat (dumpy) telescope attached to it
tilt:	a canvas covering
catenary curve:	the curve of a chain
left off his pole:	all hairdressers used to have a striped pole as their shop-sign. Percomb does not have one because he thinks he is superior to the rest
flitches:	bacon or pork
Sophoclean:	Sophocles (c.496–406BC) was a Greek poet who wrote tragedies, among them *Oedipus* and *Antigone*
pomace:	what is left of apples after the juice has been pressed out of them

Chapter 2

With two guineas Percomb tries to buy locks of Marty South's hair for Mrs Charmond, who is going overseas and wants to look her best for the next lover. Marty's father, fearful that a tree will kill him, lies ill in bed.

NOTES AND GLOSSARY:

bill-hook:	a heavy knife with an end curved for pruning
spars:	sharpened pegs of wood used by thatchers
court-roll:	a tenant's copy of the title to his property
cotter:	peasant
impression-picture:	the girl's hair is highlighted to the exclusion of everything else about her, as in an Impressionist painting
Doctor Faustus:	in the plays of Christopher Marlowe, the English dramatist (1564–93), and Goethe, the German author (1712–1832), he is the protagonist who sells his soul to the Devil for power. Marty knows the story from a cheap edition, 'the penny book'
vamped:	walked
lifehold:	the property is South's as long as he lives

Chapter 3

During the night Marty stores her spars in the waggon-house of George Melbury who cannot sleep for thinking of his well-educated daughter Grace whom he wants the impecunious Giles Winterborne to marry. Because Melbury was married by a trick to the woman Giles's father loved, he wants to make up for it by marrying Grace to Giles. It is a sacrifice. Marty, having overheard Melbury's plan, goes home to cut off her hair because she loves Giles, and now there is no point in looking attractive.

NOTES AND GLOSSARY:

ante-mundane: before the world as we know it

Ginnung-Gap: a vast abyss in Teutonic mythology. Hardy is emphasising the emptiness and barrenness of Marty's life

turnpike bonds: Melbury has bought bonds from a Trust whose business it is to maintain roads and whose revenue comes from tolls at turnpike gates

Nature does not ... storm: old age makes it difficult for the heart to protect itself from the blasts of life

celandines: perennial herbs with bright yellow flowers

'buffeting ... storm': from 'The Small Celandine' (1802) by William Wordsworth (1770–1850)

Loke the Malicious: in Norse mythology he was an evil god who cut off the hair of Thor's wife

gads: sticks

Chapter 4

A day in the life of the woodlanders begins as they gossip about Mrs Charmond while they work. They consider her a woman of easy virtue, and Grace a young lady who has been kept at school too long. Dr Fitzpiers arouses their suspicion because he is fond of science, philosophy, and poetry. Melbury explains to the workmen that he is proud of his daughter because she has had an education he never had. A business arrangement prevents his meeting Grace who is on her way home from the boarding school. He asks Giles to meet her at Sherton market. He hopes they will marry, but thinks Grace too good for Giles.

NOTES AND GLOSSARY:

crib-framing: a crib is a rack or manger containing food for animals (sheep-cribs are referred to in the previous chapter)

copse-ware: goods made of wood

Hapsburgian:	the royal family of Austria, the Hapsburgs, gained control of much of Europe through intermarriages
journeymen:	workers who have a craft or trade
etiolated:	lacking vigour
hollow-turnery:	the making of hollow wooden utensils like bowls
pit:	one man stands in the saw-pit, the other stands above it, and between them they saw the piece of wood that is attached to a frame
knee-jints:	knee-joints
tell off . . . money:	say your prayers as quickly and as glibly as a businessman counting money
victuals . . . that:	she dines in a low-cut dress
beater:	an old watch with a good solid tick or beat
pattens:	wooden overshoes worn by women to keep their feet dry
teuny:	puny
huffed:	bullied
nesh:	fragile, sickly

who dragged whom . . . ?: the Greek hero Achilles dragged the body of Hector, son of King Priam, around the walls of Troy as an act of vengeance

victual your carcase: feed yourself

Chapter 5

Giles goes to meet Grace at Sherton Abbas. Ironically, on the way he meets Marty who is delivering her locks of hair to the barber. She learns that should her father die their house becomes Mrs Charmond's property. Grace in her finery, and Giles holding his apple tree, meet awkwardly at the market. Marty, assuming that they are drawn to one another as kindred souls, and wishing to avoid them, walks home part of the way until Mrs Charmond's carriage gives her a lift.

On the way to the market she met the reason for keeping her hair; on the way home she meets the reason for losing it.

NOTES AND GLOSSARY:

perruquier:	maker of wigs
bain't:	am not
transcendentalism:	a state of being visionary and idealistic
reductio ad absurdum **. . .:**	(*Latin*) a proof of the absurdity
Prout's or Vandyke brown:	Hardy enhances her importance and beauty by thinking of her eyebrows painted in brown – a colour associated with the painters Samuel Prout (1783 – 1852) and Anthony van Dyck (1599–1641)

poll:	head
Olympian:	like the home of the gods
Tempe-vale:	a beautiful valley in Greece
fay:	succeed

Chapter 6

Hardy draws a contrast between the 'woodland sequestration' of Giles and the urban sophistication of Grace as they ride home behind Mrs Charmond's carriage. The Melbury family, absorbed in their daughter, forget Giles who is outside and who goes away thinking of Grace and Marty. Grace is fascinated by a light from the doctor's house because it is unusual and interrupts 'the regular terrestrial roll which produced the season's changes'. After her chat with Grammer Oliver she thinks of the young doctor as a man of advanced ideas, probably destined for higher things.

NOTES AND GLOSSARY:

gipsying:	having a picnic
jambs:	doorposts
jine:	join
projick:	prodigy
rozums:	quaint sayings
as a natomy:	for anatomy
chick, chiel:	children

Chapter 7

Melbury and daughter, followed by Giles Winterborne, walk through dead and crippled woodland to an auction. Giles, who cannot keep his eyes off Grace, buys wood he does not need and unwittingly bids against her father. Later when he calls on the Melburys Giles is again left out in the cold as Grace prepares herself for the visit to the House of Mrs Charmond.

NOTES AND GLOSSARY:

in which . . . foliage: the leaves stayed on the trees longer
pari passu: (*Latin*) keeping step
Jarnvid wood: an iron wood of spears in Norse mythology
faggots: bundles of twigs
Peripatetic, Lyceum: Aristotle (384–322 B.C.), the Greek philosopher, used to teach students at the Lyceum school in Athens. It was his habit to walk up and down while lecturing. For that reason his school was called 'peripatetic' (*Greek*, walk about)

| spray: | twigs, kindling |
| cheval glass: | a mirror big enough to reflect the whole figure |

Chapter 8

Mrs Charmond, with her almond eyes and sophisticated manner, wins Grace's confidence and invites her on a sentimental journey to Europe. Giles and Marty plant pine trees. He sees Grace returning from Mrs Charmond's and sees the young doctor watching her through an eyeglass over the hedge across the road.

NOTES AND GLOSSARY:

laps:	overlapping of slates on a roof
rolls:	the overlaps are rolled to make them waterproof
mullion:	the thin upright in the framework of a window
hood:	a canopy over a window
ashlar:	masonry of square hewn stones
plinth:	the projecting part of a wall just above the ground
gin:	trap
Sentimental Journey:	*A Sentimental Journey through France and Italy* (1768), a witty account of travels in Europe by Laurence Sterne (1713–68), whose major work is *Tristram Shandy*
lucubrations:	studies
weltbürgerliche:	*(German)* cosmopolitan

Chapter 9

When Grace talks about Mrs Charmond with such respect, Giles feels that he is just a peasant who plants trees. He wonders if anything can come of their relationship but is relieved to hear her say that she loves Hintock and its people 'fifty times better than all the Continent'. Marty encourages Giles to have a Christmas party so that his hypothetical man and maid will get to know one another better by dancing. Melbury vows on John Winterborne's headstone to make amends for the wrong he did in marrying his woman. To the embarrassment of Giles, the Melbury family arrives early and helps prepare for the party. Grace seems at ease though she is not pleased when furniture-polish stains her dress.

NOTES AND GLOSSARY:

Moses . . . Mount:	Grace's face is shining (see Exodus 34:29)
Dumas:	Alexandre Dumas (1802–70) was a writer of romantic novels and travel books
Méry:	François Méry (1797–1866) wrote some travel books

a-croupied:	crouched
Beelzebub:	the Devil
randyvoo:	party (from the French *rendezvous*)
skiver:	to skewer, truss up
bruckle het:	a changeable heat (literally); a great pity

Chapter 10

The next mishap is the splashing of stew on Grace's face. The woodlanders play with the new cards; the rest of the company with old stained cards. Giles is not having much luck. And then Melbury stands with his back to the fire as though he owned the place. Grace, thinking of new dances in large houses, does not join in. To the fortune teller her father says: 'You can't teach her anything new. She's been too far among the wise ones to be astonished at anything she can hear among us folks in Hintock.' It is as though she belongs to another world. Her education has alienated her from her background. It is ironical then that Melbury should say of Dr Fitzpiers because he is educated: 'I don't expect he'll stay here long.' Melbury knows that she does not belong with Giles and the woodlanders. Giles feels that he has lost Grace for ever – especially when Robert Creedle tells of the slug on her plate.

NOTES AND GLOSSARY:

Flemish Last-Suppers:	Hardy is thinking of the draperies in Flemish paintings of Christ's Last Supper
hang-fairs:	public executions
langterloo:	a simple gambling game
mien . . . matters:	looking very self-important
superficies:	surface
phrenologists:	people who study the shape of the skull and draw conclusions about the development of the various faculties in the individual
holler:	hollow
sperrits:	spirits
criddled:	curdled
randys:	parties (see note on 'randyvoo' in Chapter 9)

Chapter 11

A crisis approaches. Grace should not marry Giles because he is a cider-merchant, apple-farmer, and woodsman and because she is an educated woman with other interests. Yet Melbury is attempting to arrange the marriage because of his vow over the grave of Giles's father. Mrs Melbury thinks Grace will marry Giles as 'an understood thing'. Grace believes she should marry him because she is promised to him. Giles arrives with a new horse to impress his beloved and interrupts the Melbury family's morning arrangements. Melbury remains unhappy. He does not want his daughter to sink down to the level of the locals in manners and in ways of speaking.

NOTES AND GLOSSARY:

shail-and-wamble: an awkward shuffling walk characteristic of the woodlanders

post hoc argument: a false argument. Grace went to Giles Winterborne's party. Mrs Charmond does nothing about seeing Grace. Melbury then concludes that Mrs Charmond disapproves of Grace keeping such low company

Chapter 12

A fox trots past Grace and her father on their morning walk. A huntsman comes upon them, asks if they shouted out to indicate that they had spotted the fox, and abuses them for not doing so. Melbury is ashamed and resentful that anybody should address his daughter in such a manner. Had he himself looked like a gentleman, it would not have happened. His daughter must have a gentleman, not a woodsman. Melbury is now determined that Grace marry well; Grace is uneasy, not wanting to be the social hope of the family, and not wanting at this time to devote her life to Giles. Tension mounts. A crisis is imminent. Her father wants her to be a social success 'though in direct antagonism to a better feeling which had hitherto prevailed with him, and had, indeed, only succumbed that morning during the ramble.' A hunter has ensured that his vow has gone to earth.

Grace feels that she is being treated as a piece of property. Her father has invested in her and looks for a return for his money. She is not to see Giles without her father's knowledge.

When Melbury learns that Mrs Charmond leaves for foreign parts the next day, he thinks that Grace is not invited because she joined the common people at Giles Winterborne's Christmas party. Creedle intensifies the gloomy and ominous tone of this chapter by announcing that should the ailing John South die, Giles Winterborne's property falls into the hands of the mistress at Hintock House.

NOTES AND GLOSSARY:

Actaeonic: hunting. The reference is not appropriate since this hunter, unlike Actaeon, the Greek hunter, has not seen a goddess bathing, nor is he likely to be torn to pieces by his own dogs as punishment as Actaeon was when he saw Diana bathing

buffer: fool
shouting a view-halloo: shouting that you had seen the fox
hobbing and nobbing: associating
blade: fellow
poet: the Greek author Menander (341–290BC)
knick-knacks: personal possessions such as pieces of furniture, ornaments, Toby jugs, and so on
chattel: possession
my wind-pipe . . . : my mouth and throat are as furry as a chimney with its coating of soot

---

Chapter 13

Giles prunes the elm tree that Marty's father fears; Grace cuts off Giles; Mrs Charmond embarks for Europe.

NOTES AND GLOSSARY:
wring-house: a shed where apples are crushed
vallie: value
squat: crush
Gregorian: ritual, church music introduced by Pope Gregory I
fugleman: a soldier who is good at drill and is imitated by other soldiers when they are learning
bill-hook: see note in Chapter 2
Niflheim: in Scandinavian mythology this was the dreary home of those who had died of sickness. Giles stays up the tree instead of pursuing Grace. It amounts to an act of self-destruction. He is heading for the gloomy fogland of death
skid: brake
trumpery: trashy, useless, without value
cock-watching: up so early
tournure: (*French*) appearance

Chapter 14

Giles examines the legal possibility of extending the lease on his house. Hardy introduces Edred Fitzpiers with his dark, intelligent eyes and air of a philosopher rather than a dandy. He recommends that the elm be chopped down to save South's life. When South sees that the tree has gone he has a fit and dies of shock the same night. The doctor shows an interest in Grace.

NOTES AND GLOSSARY:
copyholds: secure and permanent property

Gideon: a reference to the Bible, Judges 7: 18–20. Gideon
                       freed the Israelites from oppression
de rigueur: (French) required for the sake of politeness

Chapter 15

Mrs Charmond insists on the letter of the law and intends pulling down
the houses; Melbury urges Giles to break off his engagement to Grace
since he has no home for her; Giles gives Grace his horse; Marty writes
on the wall:

O Giles, you've lost your dwelling-place,
And therefore, Giles, you'll lose your Grace

Grace, warming to Giles, alters the 'lost' to 'keep' in a rash mood.
Thinking that he saw her change the writing, Grace hopes that their
engagement will continue. The letter of Giles to Melbury destroys that
wish. 'Fate, it seemed, would have it this way, and there was nothing to
do but to acquiesce.' Giles did not see her and withdraws into himself.

NOTES AND GLOSSARY:
divinity who shaped the ends: an allusion to Shakespeare's *Hamlet*
monthly rose: the India or China Rose that is erroneously
                       supposed to flower every month
plenary absolution: a complete acquittal. Giles is no longer tied to
                       Grace in any way

Chapter 16

Fitzpiers sees Grace for the second time. Hardy strikes a warning note
when he describes the doctor as preferring the ideal world to the real.
For him love is a feeling of joy 'which we project against any suitable
object in the line of our vision'. Grace happens to open a gate, he sees
her, and that feeling attaches itself to her. Giles is reluctant to tell him
who she is but Fitzpiers finds out anyway when he sees her at a window
of the Melbury house. She remains in his thoughts. Giles thinks they
have something in common.

NOTES AND GLOSSARY:
'She moved upon this earth . . . ': from the poem 'The Revolt of Islam',
                       Canto II, stanza 23, by Percy Bysshe Shelley
                       (1792–1822)
Leyden jar: device for storing and discharging electricity
                       invented by Cuneus of Leyden in 1746
Spinoza: a philosopher (1632–77) who believed that virtue is
                       its own reward

ipsa hominis essentia: (*Latin*) the very essence of man

Socratic . . . : the Greek philosopher Socrates (469–399BC) used irony as his main teaching method. Feigning ignorance he would ask apparently naïve questions to arrive at the truth

'who . . . garment': from the Bible, Proverbs 30:4

Chapter 17

The ailing Grammer Oliver begs Grace to go to Fitzpiers and ask him to destroy the contract she has made willing her head to the medical profession. Grace is embarrassed about calling on the young man and is afraid that he will insist that the contract be honoured. Hardy points out that it was by chance that the doctor was interested in anatomy that month. His interests change rapidly and he has too many hobbies to become expert at any one. Lonely and isolated in Hintock, he starts to imagine an ideal mistress. Outer surroundings have no appeal for him so he turns to his inner world and imagines Grace 'ready and willing to be wooed by himself and nobody else'. He falls asleep thinking that he is made for higher things and that any acquaintance with Grace must be casual.

NOTES AND GLOSSARY:

'Ch woll: I will
wherrit: worry
chevy: chase
chimmer: bedroom
Zodiac: a calendar in astronomy or astrology, based on the positions of twelve star constellations such as Aries (the ram), Taurus (the bull), etc

---

Chapter 18

Grace finds him handsome and asleep. As he dreams of her his eyes open imagining that Grace is in the room. She leaves, he coaxes her back, destroys the contract, and flatters her. His idea of the ideal woman has now found a body where it belongs. Grace, flattered to be called a 'lovely creature', is also assured that he could never deceive her. Hardy intrudes with an ominous and melodramatic statement: 'Foreknowledge to the distance of a year or so, in either of them, might have spoilt the effect of that pretty speech.'

NOTES AND GLOSSARY:

supplicatory mandate: Fitzpiers begs and commands Grace to enter
rodomontade: boasting, exaggeration

Chapter 19

Fitzpiers has no intention of marrying Grace. She will relieve his monotonous life. After spending some time with the workmen who are barking the trees he wonders if he could settle down in Hintock and marry Grace. By chance she arrives in her father's gig and later he helps her find her purse. On learning of a previous admirer's offer of marriage and his rejection, Fitzpiers shows that he would like to make such a proposal. Grace tells Marty that Giles Winterborne is nothing to her.

NOTES AND GLOSSARY:

bark:	Melbury sold bark for tanning
'little toilette':	shaving the victim's neck before he is beheaded
apple-blooth:	apple blossom
setting:	forming of the fruit
shy little bird:	nightingale
Crusoe's island:	a reference to Daniel Defoe's (1660–1731) novel *Robinson Crusoe* (1719–20)
Schleiermacher:	a German theologian (1768–1834)

Chapter 20

The young girls of the district sow hempseed to cast a spell that will reveal their future husbands to them. Fitzpiers catches Grace in his arms and declares that he will keep her there for ever. Within minutes he chases Suke Damson for a kiss. It is daybreak when they return. Grammer Oliver predicts that Grace and Fitzpiers will marry. She thinks that Grace should marry Giles and that the doctor should marry Mrs Charmond. The voice of truth usually comes from Hardy's rustics or woodlanders.

NOTES AND GLOSSARY:

midsummer eve:	a delightful traditional festival on the eve of the longest day of this year
larries:	fun and games
tole:	entice
hoydenish:	having the manners of an ill-bred woman – lively and earthy
'. . . Foggy, foggy dew':	a traditional ballad which Suke sings to issue a sexual invitation

Chapter 21

A short fat man in evening dress is escorted by Giles to Hintock House where he seeks, without success, Mrs Charmond.

NOTES AND GLOSSARY:

the Southern cause: the American Civil War (1861–4). Southern fought Northern states for their freedom. The upshot was that slavery was abolished and the states were united

Chapter 22

Although Grace has never thought of Fitzpiers as her destined husband, she agrees to permit him to court her.

NOTES AND GLOSSARY:

'What maggot has the gaffer ...': what is worrying the boss now? 'To have a bee in one's bonnet' is a similar expression

sommit ... chiel: something to do with his child

flung your grapnel: trapped

dram: a glass of spirits

Chapter 23

He wants a quiet marriage in a registry office because if he opens a medical practice later in Budmouth he thinks people should not know of her humble origins.

NOTES AND GLOSSARY:

crochet: in Gothic architecture crochet capitals are stylised leaves

Galen, Hippocrates, Herophilus: famous ancient Greek physicians whose methods were dogmatic, empiric and hermetical: that is, based on accepted truths, based on experience, and based on alchemy

Interpreter's: Hardy alludes to *The Pilgrim's Progress* (1678) by John Bunyan (1628–88)

uppingstock: steps for mounting a horse

Chapter 24

Grace sees Suke Damson leave the house of Fitzpiers early in the morning. The explanation he gives is that Suke wanted a tooth out. Grace believes him and agrees to marry him provided the ceremony takes place in a church. Giles has disappeared from the scene. They marry.

NOTES AND GLOSSARY:

in the pouts: sulking

recalcitration: objection
carking: irritating

Chapter 25

Grace, who enjoys the old-fashioned woodland activities, is pleased to see Giles, the travelling cider-maker, at work outside the hotel where she is staying at the end of her honeymoon. She thinks that 'pressure of events' prevented her from marrying Giles. Fitzpiers, who despises the woodlanders, now loses their respect because he has married one of them. He had to choose between Grace and his career. Tense and disturbed, he goes to attend on Mrs Charmond who has had an accident. A marriage of two months is in danger.

NOTES AND GLOSSARY:
mullioned: see note in Chapter 8
'marvellous boy':   the phrase comes from Wordsworth's poem 'Resolution and Independence' and refers to Thomas Chatterton (1752–70) whose verses from *Oella* have just been quoted in the text
mawn-baskets: deep, round, wicker baskets with two handles
pomace: see note in Chapter 1
Pomona's plain: she was the Roman goddess of fruit trees
hopper: the container which passes grain to the machinery
contemporary poet: Edmund Gosse (1849–1928) whose poem 'Two Points of View' Giles Winterborne would not have read
locum tenens: (*Latin*) literally, holding the place. When a doctor is on holiday he appoints a locum to take his place temporarily
relieving officer: official in charge of relief for the poor
handwriting on the wall: strange writing on the wall at Belshazzar's Feast. See the Bible, Daniel 5
Board of Guardians: the governing body of the Union

Chapter 26

There is a bond between Fitzpiers and Mrs Charmond, who first met at Heidelberg where he was a student. The doctor becomes obsessed with the fascinating woman.

NOTES AND GLOSSARY:
pinion: gable
to still greater obliquity: the apple trees are bent right over with the weight of the fruit

| phaeton: | a light, open carriage |
| *trouvaille*: | (*French*) a lucky find |

Chapter 27

To be near Mrs Charmond, Fitzpiers refuses the practice in Budmouth, only to discover that she is going to Middleton Abbey. She realises the irony of the situation. If her agent had assented to Giles Winterborne's request to keep his house, Grace would have married him, and she could have had Fitzpiers.

NOTES AND GLOSSARY:

gold-beater's skin: used as sticking plaster, but Fitzpiers prefers the black because it is conspicuous
coquet: flirt
Neckar: a river that flows through Heidelberg
Achillean moodiness: Agamemnon offended Achilles, the great hero of Homer's *Iliad*, who withdrew from the Trojan War to sulk in his tent
the folding star: the evening star that was the sign for sheep to be brought home to the fold

Chapter 28

Grace learns that Fitzpiers is visiting Mrs Charmond at Middleton Abbey 'and she wondered if there were one world in the universe where the fruit had no worm, and marriage no sorrow.' Giles knows about their secret meetings too. Grace now knows what she has lost in rejecting Giles.

NOTES AND GLOSSARY:

crossing: being astride
'hag-rid': ridden by a witch
Tannhäuser: German minstrel invited to live with Venus, goddess of love
'Towards the loadstar': the lines are by Shelley (1792–1822)
Wouvermans: a Dutch artist (1620–88) who excelled at painting white horses
malic acid: acid from apples
cairn: a pile of stones that are often erected as a memorial to somebody or something
logan-stones: large rocks peculiarly balanced on their bases so that the hand may move them slightly. The best known of these rocking stones is in Cornwall
for the nonce: for the time being

Chapter 29

By chance Grace discovers that Suke Damson has never had a tooth pulled. Her husband is a liar, a cheat, and a snob. The marriage has been a frightful mistake. In pleasing her father she has degraded herself. Hardy's description of the disfigured, half-dead oak emphasises her feeling of desolation. Fitzpiers, sound asleep on the back of the mare, is suddenly awakened and lets slip the name 'Felice'.

NOTES AND GLOSSARY:

hollow-turner:	see note in Chapter 4
spigots:	pegs for plugging the holes in barrels
Absalont:	Absalom, son of David, whose forces defeated him, fled on a mule. His long hair caught in an oak-tree and the enemy caught and killed him. See the Bible, 2 Samuel 18, 6–15
Millamant:	the witty heroine who enjoys a conquest in *The Way of the World* (1700), a light-hearted comedy by William Congreve (1670–1729)
veil of Isis:	to lift the veil of Isis, the Egyptian goddess associated with sexuality and nature, is to reveal a fascinating and great mystery
whilom:	previously
raft:	worry

Chapter 30

As autumn comes to an end, Mrs Charmond returns to Hintock House, Melbury is determined to fight for Grace, and Fitzpiers gives up studying at night. Grace finds that she admires Giles more and more for his 'honesty, goodness, manliness, tenderness, devotion', and that these qualities are much more important to her than the tastes she acquired through an education. She refuses to act on her father's suggestion that she call on Mrs Charmond, and wishes she had never been sent to school. She hates the genteel life. Grace belongs with the woodlanders.

NOTES AND GLOSSARY:

'As one ... ':	Shakespeare's *Hamlet*, Act III, Scene ii
unguibus et rostro:	(*Latin*) with claws and beak
peck:	a great deal

Chapter 31

Rumours spread. Melbury tells Giles the whole story of the disastrous marriage and assures him that Grace still loves him.

NOTES AND GLOSSARY:

Coventry:	the husband of Lady Godiva (1040–80) jokingly said that he would remit the tax he had imposed on people in Coventry if she rode naked through the streets during the day. She ordered the townspeople not to look. There were no more taxes
Ariadne:	in Greek mythology Ariadne, the daughter of the King of Crete, rescued Theseus from the Labyrinth after he had slain the Minotaur (a monster – half bull, half man). He married and later deserted her
Vashti:	the Persian king Ahasuerus divorced his wife Vashti for refusing to reveal her beauty to his guests
Amy Dudley:	the wife of Robert Dudley, Earl of Leicester, Queen Elizabeth's favourite. She was found dead at the foot of some stairs. It was thought that Dudley had killed her because he wanted to marry the queen
Cain:	Genesis 4. Cain killed his brother Abel

Chapter 32

Melbury calls on Felice Charmond and delivers the finest speech of his life in which he pleads with her to cast off Fitzpiers for the sake of his daughter's happiness. He leaves. A Continental gentleman calls. Refusing to see him, and in a state of great agitation, she goes for a walk. She is particularly distressed to learn that she hurt Grace by not continuing their friendship.

NOTES AND GLOSSARY:

femme de trente ans: (*(French)*) woman of thirty years
édition définitive: (*French*) standard edition; the final version

Chapter 33

Grace comes upon Giles Winterborne and his men clearing the undergrowth. After a brief, friendly conversation he withdraws on seeing Mrs Charmond approaching. It is Grace's turn to deliver a fine speech. There is recrimination, anguish, and eventual understanding when the women spend the night lost in the woods. Mrs Charmond is not toying with Fitzpiers. She loves him but promises to do her best not to see him. Grace comes out with her finest line so far: 'You may see him as much as you like – for me.'

NOTES AND GLOSSARY:

noctambulist:	night-walker
verbatim:	(*Latin*) word for word

Chapter 34

Fitzpiers returns from London to find his practice dwindling even more and a letter from Felice Charmond begging him not to see her again. Grace is staying with an acquaintance. He overhears the local people talking about Mrs Charmond's planned departure, and prophesying the benefit her absence will be to a certain married couple. Mary South gives him a letter revealing the source of Felice's hair. Melbury rides to Hintock House where he sees Felice and his son-in-law parting. In the shade of the oak tree Fitzpiers rides away on the wrong horse and Melbury is left with Darling, the mare Giles gave his daughter. Melbury comes across him, thrown from his horse and asking for help which he gets in the form of rum.

NOTES AND GLOSSARY:
Mother of the Months: the moon
woak: oak
tinkling simples: tinkling cymbals (see the Bible, 1 Corinthians 13:1)
                    meaning, without charity we are nothing

Chapter 35

No breakfast and rum make Fitzpiers talk. He hates Hintock and its people, he is not appreciated, he is a man of education, he has married beneath him, he wishes he had seen the other woman first. His wife is ill, and if anything happened to her, his freedom, fame and happiness would be guaranteed. Melbury throws him from the horse. Suke Damson and Felice Charmond hasten in alarm to the doctor's house. Rumour has it that he has been seriously injured. Where is Fitzpiers?

NOTES AND GLOSSARY:
Pro—Pre—:   in Greek mythology Prometheus, who stole fire
                    from heaven, was chained to a rock on Mount
                    Caucasus where an eagle ate his liver
freak: prank, caper
Revelation: See the Bible, Revelation 6:8
Psalm of Asaph: See the Bible, Psalms 73:14
bien aimé: (*French*) well beloved
skirr: grating

Chapter 36

Felice makes preparation for leaving the district when Fitzpiers, half-dead, knocks at the window. She cleans the blood from his face and from the fence, she wines and dines him and finds him a bed. He writes a farewell letter to Grace. Fitzpiers cannot live in the same house as Melbury who has shown him such animosity. Of course Melbury thought he was unhurt when he got up and walked away.

NOTES AND GLOSSARY:

Montagu:	Lady Mary Wortley Montagu (1720–1800), a leader of London society in the eighteenth century. She was a prolific writer of letters, and had some literary talent. Of her, Dr Johnson (1709–84), the distinguished lexicographer and critic, wrote: 'She diffuses more knowledge than any woman I know, or, indeed, almost any man'
Sudarium:	cloth for wiping off sweat
St Veronica:	she offered Christ, on his way to Calvary, a towel to wipe his face. Christ's features were imprinted on it. The face of Fitzpiers is pale and covered with blood – like Christ's
concatenation:	chain

not poppy not mandragora: from Shakespeare's *Othello* Act III Scene iii. Fitzpiers means that nothing can cure the rift between Melbury and himself

the veil of that temple . . . ': when Christ died the curtain over the tabernacle in the Temple of Jerusalem was torn in two (Matthew 27). Fitzpiers thinks that what he said to Melbury has had catastrophic results

---

Chapter 37

Fitzpiers, then Felice, leave for the Continent. At the market the broken-hearted Melbury meets Fred Beaucock who persuades him that under a new law divorce is easy and that his daughter should soon be a free woman. Giles remains dubious about Melbury's conviction that he can have Grace soon if he wants her. Suffering a nervous attack, Grace's health deteriorates. In a letter from London her father assures her that she will be divorced soon, and thus freed from her exhausting fears.

NOTES AND GLOSSARY:

Valley of Humiliation:	Melbury is ashamed, humiliated. Again the allusion is to Bunyan's *Pilgrim's Progress*
new law:	a change in the divorce law
nipperkin:	a small measure of liquor
Council:	Melbury is so pleased at the turn of events that he looks transported like an angel, as St Stephen did when he faced his accusers on the Jewish Council. See the Bible, Acts 6–7

Chapter 38

Giles, who cannot believe that he will be able to make Grace happy, meets her at the Sherton market and joins her in the Abbey. It is clear that they love one another. They know they must wait for legal matters to be settled.

NOTES AND GLOSSARY:

ceorl:	churl, somebody of the lowest class
pharmacopoeia:	book containing a list of drugs and medicines
Arcadian:	they sound like people from Arcadia, a mythological region where all is bliss and contentment
recrudescence:	the breaking out again of her fastidiousness

Chapter 39

Melbury urges Grace to make sure of winning Giles. Giles's conscience troubles him. It suffers a severe blow when in the heat of the moment, he succumbs to a passionate embrace. Giles already knows that divorce proceedings have failed. Grace finds out from her father; Giles could not summon up the courage to tell her.

NOTES AND GLOSSARY:

Desdemona:	in Shakespeare's *Othello* Act III, Scene iv

Chapter 40

Fitzpiers writes asking Grace to meet him in Budmouth at the pier in three days and to return with him across the Channel. She does not go. As the carriage of Fitzpiers approaches the Melbury house, she runs away through the woods to find Giles to escort her to a friend's house.

NOTES AND GLOSSARY:

intramural:	within walls
stint myself:	live frugally, deny myself
'drong':	narrow lane
Daphnean instinct:	she feels like avoiding a lover's pursuit, just as Daphne fled from the god Apollo
'Long tears ... ':	from 'A Ballad of Life' by Algernon Swinburne (1837–1909)

Chapter 41

The rain pours down. They cannot go on. Giles offers her his hut and stays in a primitive shelter nearby. Weak and feverish, he is consoled by the fact that there was 'one man on earth in whom she believed absolutely, and he was that man'. Because Grace is still married, it is a point of honour that they keep apart. She envies the small creatures wandering around the hut. They know nothing of law and sin. As the storm rages outside she starts to think that Giles may not be well. Desperately she shouts: 'Come to me, dearest! I don't mind what they say or what they think of us any more.'

This chapter has dramatic urgency as the pace of the narrative increases, and a climax approaches.

NOTES AND GLOSSARY:
buttery: stores

Chapter 42

She has not seen Giles for a day when she hears a cough. 'Can it be that cruel propriety is killing the dearest heart that ever woman clasped to her own!' The sentiment is melodramatic; the illness of Giles is real. Within fifty yards she finds him flushed and delirious. She manages to get him back to the hut where she nurses him as best she can. Grace is stricken with anguish and guilt because she might have been the cause. She feels reverence for Giles because of his lonely self-sacrifice. The only doctor in the district is Fitzpiers who readily agrees to Grace's request to tend a man who is dangerously ill.

NOTES AND GLOSSARY:
eft: newt
ichthyosauri: prehistoric, grotesque, carnivorous animals
shock: stook. Sheaves of corn are placed upright leaning on one another to dry. A space is thus formed in the middle
Aphrodite: in Grace there is more of Artemis (chastity) than there is of Aphrodite (love)

Chapter 43

Giles dies. As punishment, Grace allows Fitzpiers to think she has been sleeping with Giles. Her father learns the truth from Marty South. Grace returns to her father's house on the understanding that her husband will leave. Fitzpiers is hoping for forgiveness.

The letter Marty South had given the doctor about Mrs Charmond's hair caused a quarrel between them, and Fitzpiers left her, unaware that her frustrated American lover was to cause another quarrel and kill them both.

NOTES AND GLOSSARY:
Psalter: book of Psalms

glutch:	stifle
Herbert:	George Herbert (1593–1663), an English religious poet

Chapter 44

Through their love for Giles the two women become close friends. Grace says that Marty should have married him because they always did everything together; Marty thinks not, because they never talked of love. Fitzpiers learns of Giles's sacrifice in giving up the hut.

NOTES AND GLOSSARY:

febrifuge:	a medicine to cool a fever
Elijah:	she thinks that Fitzpiers was showing off his skill as Elijah was in the Bible, 2 Kings 1

Chapter 45

Grace gets a love letter from Fitzpiers. He begs to see her. Grace, wanting a medical opinion on her share in the death of Giles, agrees to meet him. Fitzpiers comes upon the wedding party of Suke Damson and Tim Tangs. When they meet, Fitzpiers warbles like an inane love-bird declaring that his love has become less passionate and more profound. Melbury also surprises the reader when he says that he will never advise his daughter again. She is her own mistress.

NOTES AND GLOSSARY:

Cymbeline:	see Shakespeare's play Act IV, Scene ii, 218–20: 'With fairest flowers Whilst summer lasts and I live here, Fidele, I'll sweeten thy sad grave . . . '
'nature is fine . . . ':	the allusion is to Shakespeare's *Hamlet* Act IV, Scene v, 161–3
modus vivendi:	(*Latin*) way of living
het across:	cut across country
lachrymose:	tearful

Measure for Measure: see Shakespeare's play Act III, Scene ii, 159–60

Chapter 46

At the next meeting Grace tells Fitzpiers that she feels betrothed to and worships Giles. Her heart is in his grave. Fitzpiers watches her house by night and is watched by Tim Tangs whose marriage is a complete failure. Tim resents Suke's continued interest in the doctor and sets a man-trap the night before they leave for New Zealand.

NOTES AND GLOSSARY:

'frustrate ghost':	from Browning's (1812–89) poem 'The Statue and the Bust' which is about unfulfilled love
innamorato:	(*Italian*) lover
mouster:	be on our way
linhay:	a farm shed

Chapter 47

Tim sets the gruesome trap to punish Fitzpiers. Grace comes out to meet him and her dress is caught in the trap. Glad to be alive, they are happily reunited. Fitzpiers has bought a partnership in a practice in the Midlands.

NOTES AND GLOSSARY:

borne the palm:	been the most successful and popular
gins:	traps (see Chapter 8)
Amazonian:	Amazons were a mythological race of female warriors of great strength

Chapter 48

Melbury is cynical about the reconciliation. He thinks that happiness is a forlorn hope for Grace and Fitzpiers. The woodlanders talk about the absurdities of courtship and marriage. The novel ends with the idealised Marty, a pathetic figure, at the grave of Giles Winterborne. 'Whenever I plant the young larches I'll think that none can plant as you planted; and whenever I split a gad, and whenever I turn the cider wring, I'll say none could do it like you.'

NOTES AND GLOSSARY:

mossel:	morsel, a piece of something to eat
kex:	plant with a hollow, dry stalk
coling:	embracing
projick:	prodigy (see Chapter 6)
lewth:	shelter

Part 3

Commentary

Tone and mood

The Woodlanders opens on a deserted highway and closes with a death and an unhappy marriage. The tone of the novel is gloomy and heavy. Extensive woodlands 'make the wayside hedges ragged by their drip and shade', the lonely road reminds the traveller of times past, there is a 'tomb-like stillness', the evening is threatening, there is a 'sombre beauty' in the country, and it is winter. A strange barber is about strange business. Most of the action takes place in Little Hintock which is remote and rustic, and where Hardy expects high tragedy in the Greek tradition to develop from the intense passions and 'closely-knit interdependence' of its inhabitants.

Hardy's allusions are ominous too. The barber reminds Marty of the Devil tempting Dr Faustus, and when she goes out the night is the edge of a vast abyss, the Ginnung-Gap of Teutonic mythology. The novel is set in Wessex, but the allusions suggest that what is to happen will have a seriousness, a gravity, and a universality. The theme will not be restricted to time or place because what is to happen is timeless and sad. Hardy hopes that the novel will have the impact of a Sophoclean tragedy.

The natural setting creates a feeling of gloom and agony. Marty hears 'the creaking sound of two overcrowded branches in the neighbouring wood, which were rubbing each other into wounds'. It is a striking image, not only startling in itself but because it anticipates the injuries people inflict on one another and on themselves. The noises made by the trees express sorrow 'together with the screech of owls, and the fluttering tumble of some awkward wood-pigeon ill-balanced on its roosting-bough.'

The human situation, then, is associated with hardship, cruelty, loneliness, darkness, silence, and death. Characters are sometimes introduced in mist or darkness as shadowy, lonely presences, as grey shades. It is as though the reader is looking through a glass darkly. The very name Winterborne suggests that he is in for suffering. As Marty and Giles walk through the night completely isolated and self-contained with nothing to say to one another, 'their lonely courses formed no detached design at all, but were part of the pattern in the great web of human doings then weaving in both hemispheres from the White Sea to

Cape Horn'. However important people think their individual lives in *The Woodlanders*, they remain but a part of the pattern in the web of existence.

Things that appear trivial are part of this pattern, this life. For example, Marty's father is ill and obsessed with the idea that an elm tree will cause his death. His fear seems absurd, but the tree is to be the death of him, just as it kills a chance Giles Winterborne has to win Grace Melbury (Chapter 13). And South's death means that Giles loses his property to Mrs Charmond and loses Grace. He goes to the woods where he lives in a hut, falls ill, and dies. In that sense the tree is the death of Giles too.

Morning dawns on Marty and Giles as 'the bleared white visage of a sunless winter day'. The first morning in the novel appears 'like a deadborn child'. The tone of the novel, then, is grave. The atmosphere is sinister, ominous. The individuals, who are figures in the pattern of the web of life, seem destined for misery. When Marty and Giles are planting trees, she thinks that the trees are sighing because they are afraid to start life in earnest, just as people are. The strong feeling generated in the novel is that there is no hope. Even if people are destroyed, the web will be repaired and life will go on. The web, like the woods, will always be there.

The woods

Seasons come and go. The woods remain. The trees grow old, become diseased, and die. New trees grow. That is what life is about. The woods remain impassive, indifferent to their surroundings and to the little people who struggle for happiness, fail, and die. Their roots are in the history of the district, so that they conjure up memories for the woodlanders and nothing for Mrs Charmond or Fitzpiers. The Hintock woods, which provide the pastoral and melancholic setting, are part of a Nature that is indifferent and often cruel. No refreshment, consolation or delight is to be found in Hardy's country life. The woods are part of the web. They are part of the natural process which is more a song of lament than a tragedy.

As Melbury and Grace make their way through the woods (Chapter 7) they 'elbowed old elms and ashes with great forks, in which stood pools of water that overflowed on rainy days and ran down their stems in green cascades. On older trees still than these huge lobes of fungi grew like lungs. Here, as everywhere, the Unfulfilled Intention, which makes life what it is, was as obvious as it could be among the depraved crowds of a city slum. The leaf was deformed, the curve was crippled, the taper was interrupted; the lichen ate the vigour of the stalk, and the ivy slowly strangled to death the promising sapling.' There is an air of defeat and disease. Life is meant to be miserable. There is a sense of a hidden, controlling force. The woods are the life process.

At the climax of the novel (Chapter 42) Grace waits in the hut for Giles to come for his breakfast. He does not come. She sees a thrush eating alone. The leaves are brown and yellowish green. Some have been blown down by the storm before their time was due. There is an old beech looking like a large scarecrow or tramp. Up it climbs a slug. Dead boughs lie around. The stems of woodbine are dying. The setting and the mood are perfect. There is to be a death. The Hintock woods are very real, are a felt presence. At the roots of some trees are yellow fungi, while others are 'wrestling for existence, their branches disfigured with wounds resulting from their mutual rubbings and blows'. It is one of the most striking images because it expresses the spirit of *The Woodlanders* as a novel about self-inflicted wounds. Under the struggling trees are rotting stumps 'rising from their mossy setting like black teeth from green gums'. The image is grotesque, perhaps even too contrived. The effect is certainly melodramatic. Compare it with a much more natural and therefore much more telling image when Melbury and Grace are looking for Fitzpiers (Chapter 29). 'They halted beneath a half-dead oak, hollow and disfigured with white tumours, its roots spreading out like claws grasping the ground.' The picture suggests the futility of human endeavour, the struggle of clinging to life and dying in the process.

The rustics

The woodlanders belong to this natural process. Like the woods they will always be there. They are ordinary country people who live, work and die. Their life is spar-making, sawing, crib-framing and copseware manufacture. They depend on the woods for a livelihood; they are part of the natural order and they have no ambitions. Fathers and sons will be woodlanders. That is the way things are meant to be. The woodlanders provide a norm and a contrast with central characters who wish to change their station in life; the woodlanders are the traditional life of the country. They speak in a local dialect that has colour and vitality. Above all it is a natural way of speaking, however difficult it may be at times to understand. Their conversation rings true. Often the most perceptive observations come from Hardy's rustics. After his unsuccessful party, Giles Winterborne wonders if Grace, who has become accustomed to sophisticated living elsewhere, will ever be able to endure the simple life at Hintock again. Robert Creedle comes straight to the heart of the matter: 'They shouldn't have schooled her so monstrous high, or else bachelor-men shouldn't give randys, or if they do give 'em, only to their own race.' Different classes do not mix. If Grace is to live our way of life she should not have had an education. She has returned to her native Hintock with the manners and interests of another class of people.

The rustics know that conflict and suffering are inevitable. It is not that Hardy sets them up as oracles but that living close to nature they understand human nature. Hardy does not idealise them. Like the woods, they are there. (See Part 4 of these notes for an examination of the function of the woodlanders in the novel.)

Hardy's prose

An air of melancholy, of brooding gloom, hangs over *The Woodlanders*. Hardy's prose style helps to create it. His prose is formal and stiff: many of the words are strange and old-fashioned. Sentences are long and are constructed in a deliberate, precise way. The reflective nature of the prose makes the plot move slowly. His style suits his theme because the subject matter of the novel is solemn. And however irritating the number of classical, biblical, historical, literary, and mythological allusions may be, these too suit his theme and intensify the pathos of the conflicts in *The Woodlanders*.

Sometimes the novel feels static, as though Hardy were writing in a trance. There is a dreamlike quality about the novel but there is nothing dreamlike or enchanting about the woods. Nature is cruel. And if it is dreamlike, it is a sad dream, not a tragedy. Hardy helps his slow plot to move by pointing forwards at the end of a chapter. Such a technique is necessary if a novelist is writing in serial form because it creates tension and makes the reader want to read on.

Fate

The characters themselves create a sense of gloom, if not futility. When talking to Giles about love, Fitzpiers thinks that we are all 'miserable creatures of circumstance'; carried away by romantic delusion because he meets Felice Charmond for the first time since he was a student, Fitzpiers declares that the human will is powerless against predestination; Grace, tacitly agreeing with her father that she could not bear the roughness of existence with Giles, sighs as she thinks of 'the intractability of circumstances'; later, when a letter breaking off their engagement comes from Giles, she is negative and passive, thinking 'Fate, it seemed, would have it this way, and there was nothing to do but to acquiesce'; two birds quarrel, fall in hot ashes and fly away, as Marty declares 'That's the end of what is called love'; at the end Melbury has a pessimistic view of Grace's future; and Giles Winterborne always seems to expect the worst.

All of these examples may suggest that Fate or chance or

predestination is a dominating and controlling agent in the novel. Some characters say so; some of the rustic characters in Hardy's novels believe so. Hardy does not believe in Fate. The human will has power to determine its own course. People shape their own lives, determine their own fates. There is choice. There are external pressures of course. Melbury wants social advancement for Grace who is torn between her instinctive harmony with Hintock and the dislocation caused by an acquired breeding, taste, and education; Giles dies in a storm because of a moral code; Marty, thinking she has lost Giles to Grace, sacrifices herself and her hair.

Although characters are gloomy, often wretched, and more often helpless, and although they often lament their sorry lot in this brief passage of time, they are not expressing the views of their creator. They express feelings that suit the occasion that caused them. In Shakespeare's *King Lear*, for example, Gloucester, deceived by his son and tortured by others, moans:

> As flies to wanton boys, are we to th' Gods;
> They kill us for their sport.

The words express the anguish of a suffering old man; the words are right for the occasion; the words do not mean that Shakespeare believes that the Gods or Fate control our destinies. The President of the Immortals may know when the game is to finish and how it will finish, but the players determine the game.

Narrative method and point of view

Hardy does not take sides. He is not a judge or referee. Characters are allowed to grow and develop and change without Hardy's preferences being indicated. The novelist remains at a distance, objective; and yet his presence is often felt. Melbury, not wanting Giles to drag Grace down to the old Hintock way of living again, discourages Grace from seeing him and they quarrel. Hardy intrudes in a pompous, omniscient way: 'The petulance that relatives show towards each other is in truth directed against that intangible Cause which has shaped the situation no less for the offenders than the offended, but is too elusive to be discerned and cornered by poor humanity in irritated mood.' The comment is in keeping with the tone of the novel as a whole but it can irritate the reader, coming as it does from outside the plot. There is another example when Melbury tries to persuade Grace to allow Fitzpiers back into the house. Hardy describes her as an 'impressionable creature, who combined modern nerves with primitive feelings, and was doomed by such co-existence to be numbered among the distressed, and to take her scourgings to their exquisite extremity.'

The reader knows about Grace's 'modern nerves' which are the result of her education and alienation from the ways of Hintock, and the reader knows about the 'primitive feelings' she often expresses in admiration of Giles and the woods themselves. That part of Hardy's comment is unnecessary because we have seen the character of Grace in action. The second part of the comment foreshadows what is to happen and may destroy any tension or suspense the novelist has created. A final example comes after the fervent declaration of Fitzpiers to Grace that he could never deceive her. 'Foreknowledge to the distance of a year or so, in either of them, might have spoilt the effect of that pretty speech.' The reader does not want such information in advance.

Usually, however, Hardy is at a distance from his material. His narrative method is not unlike that of a film camera, and the reader often feels that he is an observer looking on at what happens in the novel, rather than being involved. It is part of Hardy's method to put the reader at a distance with him from the scene of the action. For example, in Chapter 1, Hardy's eye sees a deserted highway from the distance. On it is a lone figure. The camera moves closer to examine his appearance. A cart arrives. The camera eye joins him in the cart to look out at the approaching Hintock. The same distancing effect is achieved when the eye, through Percomb, first sees Marty South. Sometimes the camera will zoom in to examine minutely the woods and the woodlanders; at other times it will be a long shot of people in a landscape. They often look very small, dwarfed by the woods that surround and support them. You will find many examples of people watching people, of eyes watching eyes watching people in *The Woodlanders*.

Hardy has a fine eye for detail and for probing the deeper reality underneath the scenic. His descriptive method is like that of an Impressionist painter. As a whole *The Woodlanders* is a still painted scene, reflective and mournful. As onlookers we form from Hardy's words a picture of the woods and woodlanders in a timeless landscape without boundaries. Things are suggested in the painting that are to echo with significance the more we look at it – things like the traps at Mrs Charmond's house, Giles up an elm tree, Giles and autumn, a haircut, Marty at a grave. They are all part of one another; they are all related to one another. Mrs Charmond jokes to Grace about trapping men. Mrs Charmond traps Fitzpiers with Marty's hair, while a man-trap is the saving grace for Fitzpiers. The naturalness and selflessness of Giles is contrasted with the selfishness and sophistication of Fitzpiers and Mrs Charmond. Giles, slow and earnest, would not be mourned by Marty had he come down from that elm tree in the mist. He, like the others, is in the mist of an Impressionist painting that is meant to be about the quivering web of the human race.

Hardy makes us see; and he makes us see that people and their relationships are not clear cut. They are never complete and final. Grace is an example of the new type of woman who is in a perpetual state of coming into being, of vacillating, of conflict within herself. Marty and Giles have a kinship, a oneness with themselves and their surroundings which is quite unconscious. But it is not possible to say that they would have made an ideal marriage because, as Marty points out, there had never been any talk of love. They are part of the pulsing pattern in the web. Things come and go. Fitzpiers and Grace come close together, move away from one another; Mrs Charmond moves into the foreground for a minute, to be replaced by Giles or the woodlanders or Marty. Even an American toddles across the canvas. And then out of the canvas leap the woods in perpetual decay shrouding and diminishing the people who, a moment ago, seemed to dominate the picture. As we watch the painting we are reminded that the people are part of a cycle, a process, a web of existence. Touch one part and the whole network shakes.

The novel abounds with examples of scenes that highlight Hardy's ability to present and dramatise the visual: Giles and assistants make cider; the barking (Chapter 19); a morning in the life of the woodlanders (Chapter 4); the man-trap (Chapter 47); pruning an elm tree (Chapter 13); eyes in a mirror (Chapter 18); Fitzpiers disappears in the distance on an adulterous mission as Giles emerges in the foreground as autumn's brother (Chapter 28); and the most powerful section of *The Woodlanders* (Chapters 41 and 42). Hardy's intention is not to develop an argument but to paint an impression of life as he sees it in a region with which he is familiar.

Characters

Grace Melbury

The central figure in *The Woodlanders* is Grace Melbury, the country girl who has been educated. We first see her through the eyes of Marty South 'looking glorified and refined to much above her former level'. She wears new gloves over her delicate hands, she is restrained and reserved. Alongside her, under the apple-tree he carries with its 'delightful suggestion of orchards', stands Giles Winterborne (Chapter 5). Marty, having given her hair to Percomb, watches. The scene dramatises the conflict in the novel as we watch these people with 'converging destinies'. Each of them is isolated. Marty stands alone, helpless, having sacrificed her hair; Grace is self-contained, preoccupied with her own state, alone; Giles is awkward, solitary, separate.

Hardy describes Grace as being sometimes beautiful, sometimes not, depending on her health and spirits. She is pale, slim, and pliant. 'Her look expressed a tendency to wait for others' thoughts before uttering her own; possibly also to wait for others' deeds before her own doings.' She lacks punch or drive or initiative. It is as though her natural or instinctive behaviour has been cloaked by a veneer of education; natural expression and movement are paralysed. She is too gentle to speak up for herself. Her conversation with Giles is stilted and superficial as she talks about people and places. She will talk about anything except herself. She has changed. It is also the character of the Melbury family not to show strong emotion.

Home in bed, her eyes are drawn to a light coming from the new doctor's house. Grammer Oliver is sure that he is not made for higher things despite his learning; Grace's learning makes her talk above the head of Giles; she takes to Mrs Charmond because of her elegance and sophistication; she declares that she much prefers the people of Hintock to those she has experienced on the Continent. Yet she always seems out of place, as Robert Creedle finds her at the party. Out of honour she should marry Giles. Of love she says nothing. As she adjusts to life in Hintock, a marriage to Giles seems possible (Chapter 11).

But her father sees her as the social hope of the family. She should marry into a higher station. Melbury ignores a solemn promise made to Winterborne's father and chooses social position. The scene where Giles prunes the elm and Grace stands below shows the gap that now separates them (Chapter 13). 'For myself I would have married you – some day – I think. But I give way, for I am assured it would be unwise.' In fact she does not have a mind of her own. She asserts nothing. She talks as though she is quoting other people or books she has read. There is something negative and helpless about Grace Melbury. Through the eyes of Fitzpiers she appears a pleasing contradiction walking 'as delicately as if she had been bred in town, and as firmly as if she had been bred in the country.' She has a thoughtful air. It is part of her isolation that she is lost in thought.

Grace is torn between the life she used to know and still loves and the civilised life she became used to away from Hintock. She is torn between Giles and Fitzpiers. The old life is represented by Marty, Giles and the woodlanders, the new by Mrs Charmond and Fitzpiers. Hardy does not say what her choice should be. Grammer Oliver does. 'But though she's a lady in herself, and worthy of any such as he, it do seem to me that he ought to marry somebody more of the sort of Mrs Charmond, and that Miss Grace should make the best of Winterborne.' As summer declines, she feels that her fate hangs in the balance. Yet life goes on as 'the one or two woodmen who sawed, shaped, or spokeshaved on her father's premises at this inactive season of the year, regularly came and unlocked the doors in the morning, locked them in the evening, supped, leant over their garden-gates for a whiff of evening air, and to catch any last and furthest throb of news from the outer world, which entered and expired at Little Hintock like the exhausted swell of a wave in some innermost cavern of some innermost creek of an embayed sea' (Chapter 24).

Grace is awed by Fitzpiers. His knowledge, family background, beliefs and professional skill impress her. He is a superior being. But when he is unfaithful he behaves like common men and his image is shattered. She realises that she had never regarded him as a lover and is not particularly jealous (Chapter 28). It is Giles who appears at that moment and it is of Giles, whom she wronged, that she thinks most often.

Grace has a new idea of what is important and what is not. 'His homeliness no longer offended her acquired tastes.' It does not matter that he is without culture. She likes his rough country appearance and admires his 'goodness, manliness, tenderness, devotion'. Grace rejects the genteel life which has ruined her own. But she cannot because she combines 'modern nerves with primitive feelings'. She starts to warm towards Fitzpiers who misses the chance with his frigid communication; then she cools, and then there is estrangement. Misled by her misinformed father she draws closer to Giles, rejects Fitzpiers, and feels uncomfortable and out of place in a simple old inn. Grace vacillates perpetually.

With the traditional and time-honoured heaving bosom she confesses to Giles: 'You know what I feel for you – what I have felt for no other living man, what I shall never feel for a man again. But as I have vowed myself to somebody else than you, and cannot be released, I must behave as I do behave, and keep that vow.' She adheres strictly to the rules. A marriage vow is binding even though the man is unfaithful. It is a form of self-torture. Grace becomes human when she invites Giles into the hut out of the rain. Too late. Her timing is poor. Her fate is a lifetime with Fitzpiers.

Grace is too 'commonplace and straight-laced' (Hardy) to be a tragic figure. There is nothing large or expansive about her; she remains light and nervous, cut off, a solitary.

Giles Winterborne

The name 'Winterborne' suggests that Giles is in for suffering. We first meet him with Marty. He is 'a man not particularly young for a lover, nor particularly mature for a person of affairs'. His manner is reserved and restrained. He talks naturally and kindly. Giles is an honest, reliable countryman. Marty and he are as one. 'They had no remarks to make to each other, and they uttered none. Hardly anything could be more isolated or more self-contained than the lives of these two . . .'. Yet they are only part of the pattern in the web (Chapter 3). There is something resigned about Giles, as though he feels fated to do this or that. His virtues are striking, yet his general air is negative.

Giles is close to the woods and part of Marty. 'He had a marvellous power of making trees grow. Although he would seem to shovel in the earth quite carelessly there was a sort of sympathy between himself and the fir, oak, or beech that he was operating on; so that the roots took hold of the soil in a few days' (Chapter 8). He is happy with the earth. He works hard and plods along. Giles isolates himself in Nature where he belongs.

In Chapter 28 Grace sees him with new eyes. 'He looked and smelt like Autumn's very brother, his face being sunburnt to wheat-colour, his eyes blue as corn-flowers, his sleeves and leggings dyed with fruit-stains, his hands clammy with the sweet juice of apples, his hat sprinkled with pips, and everywhere about him that atmosphere of cider which at its first return each season has such an indescribable fascination for those who have been born and bred among the orchards.' The passage evokes well his positive qualities of generosity, kindness, and naturalness. Here he is at his best.

At the beginning of the novel he is too passive. He lacks drive or initiative. At home with trees and apples, he is not at ease with people. He loves Grace and wants to marry her but does not do enough to achieve his ambition. Admittedly she does not feel that she is ready to marry him yet; but he could have been more persuasive. He could have come down from the elm tree instead of staying up there in isolation. Hardy makes that point forcefully. His modesty and humility are impediments. He wants to arise from his obscurity into a married state with Grace. Time passes. He is beaten before he starts. It is as though he thinks he is fated never to win her. When Fitzpiers marries her, Giles withdraws into himself living the life of a hermit in the woods.

The possibility of a divorce does not cheer him up. He remains resigned, negative. He feels inferior to the accomplished Grace because he is unrefined. They could never be happy together for that reason. He feels guilty about kissing her since he knows the divorce is impossible. A stubborn despair and cynicism possess him. Giles is silent and withdrawn, depending on others for nothing. He is himself, alone. 'He had once worshipped her, laid out his life to suit her, wooed her and lost her.' Given a second chance he does not have the same hope. Nor will he take a positive step. 'He would even repulse her – as a tribute to conscience' (Chapter 39). Giles remains long-suffering, devoted and hopeless. 'A feverish disposition which had been hanging about him for some time, the result of a chill caught the previous winter, seemed to acquire virulence with the prostration of his hopes' (Chapter 40).

In fact the loss of Grace the second time is to be the death of him. The climax of *The Woodlanders* is the death of Giles. What happens after that is the rather tedious and unconvincing reconciliation of Grace and Fitzpiers. Giles's death is pathetic rather than tragic. He was no tragic figure, no hero. Marty's tribute is the best: 'Whenever I plant the young larches I'll think that none can plant as you planted; and whenever I split a gad, and whenever I turn the cider wring, I'll say none could do it like you. If ever I forget your name let me forget home and heaven! . . . . But no, no, my love, I never can forget 'ee; for you was a good man, and did good things!' (Chapter 48).

Edred Fitzpiers

Just as Hardy is interested in the place of an educated young woman in a rustic society, so too is he interested in the position of a professional man in country to which he is foreign. Each of them is uncomfortable. We learn from Grammer Oliver that he comes from one of the oldest families in the country, that he misses society, enjoys his books and laboratory, and thinks that he is made for higher things (Chapter 6). Fitzpiers is handsome, dark-eyed, alert, and soft-featured. He looks as though he has a depth of vision in keeping with that of a philosopher; but underneath may be a dilettante and dandy. He sounds as though he is full of ideas but he may be glib and shallow. His first action in the novel is to have the tree removed – a remedy that causes the death of Marty's father (Chapter 14).

He is attracted to Grace because there is no crude rusticity in her. It was when he was reading a German metaphysician that he saw her open a gate, and his imagination was fired. The main point that Hardy makes is that the doctor is not a practical man and prefers the ideal world to the real world. He would rather think about Grace and an alliance with her than actually pursue her. Like Hardy, he enjoys quoting Shelley, and he gives Winterborne the impression that he is in love with Grace. Fitzpiers is quick to correct that impression. Isolated and lonely, he is like a Leyden jar packed with electricity and awaiting a conductor to disperse it. For him, human love 'is joy accompanied by an idea which we project against any suitable object in the line of our vision, just as the rainbow iris is projected against an oak, ash, or elm tree indifferently'.

Any woman who crossed his line of vision while the idea of love was germinating in his head, not his heart, would have seized his attention. He claims it was chance that it happened to be Grace. And he admits that he is in love with something in his own head 'and no thing-in-itself outside it at all' (Chapter 16). Because he thinks he is destined for higher things he can contemplate only a flirtation with Grace, who is to learn too late of the real Fitzpiers and not the product of her imagination. She is to learn of 'a man of too many hobbies to show likelihood of rising to any great eminence in the profession he had chosen, or even to acquire any wide practice in the rural district he had marked out as his field of survey for the present' (Chapter 17). His senses are sharp, he is unpractical, he likes the abstract, he is impressionable. Loneliness at Hintock drives him back into his imagination, into his own inner resources where he becomes isolated from the real world outside. Fitzpiers creates for himself an ideal mistress that is Grace Melbury. She sees him as 'a specimen of creation altogether unusual in that locality'.

Above all Fitzpiers is an idealist who sees himself as having limitless possibilities and sees Grace as an exceptional person. He even talks to himself and contemplates settling down to quiet domesticity in Hintock (Chapter 19). The language Hardy uses shows that the romantic doctor's concoctions are to be dangerous potions if not airy bubbles. 'That the Idea had for once completely fulfilled itself in the objective substance . . . he was enchanted enough to fancy must be the case at last.' The words 'enchanted' and 'fancy' make the author's point of view clear. Fitzpiers is fanciful, a dreamer. His Idea of love is embodied in Grace for the time being. The Idea takes many shapes. Having pledged to love her for ever, he releases Grace, and pursues the hoydenish Suke Damson to spend the night with her in a hay-field. 'While they remained silent on the hay the coarse whirr of the eternal night-hawk burst sarcastically from the top of a tree at the nearest corner of the wood.' That is Hardy's comment on the Idea of Fitzpiers. So much for idealism (Chapter 20).

Fitzpiers regards the woodlanders as inferior beings. Near the end of the honeymoon he realises that he has sacrificed his ambition in marrying Grace, and that she who has shared his tastes and ideas is still one of the Hintock tribe. He does not wish to mix with the woodlanders. Grace is distressed that he should scorn 'woodland forms of life which in his courtship he had professed to regard with so much interest' (Chapter 25). The woodlanders no longer consider him a superior being. His medical practice falls away.

Like a butterfly he flits from one source of interest to another. In Felice Charmond he finds somebody of his own kind, and feels that they were fated to meet again. Memories of student days and romantic fantasies imbue with importance and excitement a relationship that never started. His imagination 'magnified that bygone and transitory tenderness to indescribable proportions'. The Idea in his head is a destructive agent (Chapter 26). As he rides off to visit Mrs Charmond, Grace wonders if there is a world in the universe where the fruit has no worm. In their marriage the worm in the fruit is Fitzpiers, and the conflict in herself between the girl she was and the woman she is now.

Fitzpiers confesses all to Melbury. He despises Hintock, nobody understands him because he is educated, he is a scientist without equal in

South Wessex, only one woman appreciates his work, he married beneath himself, he is ambitious, and if anything happened to Grace he would be free, happy, and would achieve fame through a union with the other woman (Chapter 35). He is speaking in the heat of passion and alcohol, but what kind of future can Grace have with this man? Has he changed after the reconciliation?

Felice Charmond

In a conversation between Marty and Percomb we learn that she is the lady from the big house. She travels, has money, and wants a head of hair for her next trip. Marty's hair, seen in church, appealed to her. The next impression is that she is a lady of easy virtue because according to Creedle, she dines in 'a gown hardly higher than her elbows' (Chapter 4). Hardy says that she has deep, mysterious eyes and a warm heart capable of imprudence (Chapter 5).

The first conversation she has with Grace is, ironically, about man-traps. She has a listless, bored air, her voice fades, her almond eyes grow larger. She prefers to smile rather than utter meanings to men. Grace is fascinated, as is Fitzpiers. 'I think sometimes I was born to live and do nothing, nothing, nothing but float about, as we fancy we do sometimes in dreams.' Mrs Charmond is a lazy dreamer whose life is enclosed within her imagination. A stranger to Hintock, she is isolated, like the doctor, and feels oppressed by her surroundings. Travelling in Europe stimulates her (Chapter 8). She is a lady with a past. A South Carolinian gentleman pursues, and eventually kills her.

Dr Fitzpiers first sees her as 'a woman of elegant figure reclining upon a couch in such a position as not to disturb a pile of magnificent hair on the crown of her head. A deep purple dressing-gown formed an admirable foil to the peculiarly rich brown of her hair-plaits; her left arm, which was naked nearly up to the shoulder, was thrown upwards, and between the fingers of her right hand she held a cigarette, while she idly breathed from her delicately curled lips a thin stream of smoke towards the ceiling' (Chapter 26). A naked arm and smoking! Not a lady! Hardy stereotypes her as an enchantress, languorous and seductive, as a woman of the world.

She is capricious and passionate. 'If one word could have expressed Felice Charmond it would have been Inconsequence. She was a woman of perversities, delighting in piquant contrasts. She liked mystery, in her life, in her love, in her history. To be fair to her, there was nothing in these which she had any great reason to be ashamed of, and many things of which she might have been proud; but her past had never been fathomed by the honest minds of Hintock, and she rarely volunteered her experiences' (Chapter 27). Hardy neither judges nor condemns her.

Indeed there is irony in that word 'honest' which suggests that the woodlanders are too simple and strait-laced to appreciate or to approve of such a colourful figure. The exception is Giles Winterborne, who gives a brief, detached account of her in Chapter 31 as a former actress, 'a bit of a charmer in her time', who married a much older man in the iron trade. He bought Hintock House and the property around it and retired there. 'A body who has smiled where she has not loved, and loved where she has not married.' Giles also says that she is generous.

When the lovers meet, their encounter is presented with a sensual intensity unusual in nineteenth-century novels. 'They looked in each other's faces without uttering a word, an arch yet gloomy smile wreathing her lips. Fitzpiers clasped her hanging hand, and, while she still remained in the same listless attitude, looking volumes into his eyes, he stealthily unbuttoned her glove, and stripped her hand of it by rolling back the gauntlet over the fingers, so that it came off inside out. He then raised her hand to his mouth, she still reclining passively, watching him as she might have watched a fly upon her dress' (Chapter 30).

A passion incarnate is what this *femme fatale* in her late twenties has become. Drawn irresistibly to Fitzpiers, she finds it hard to agree to Grace's request to release him. The manner of her removal from the plot is both unlikely and unconvincing. Her thread in the fabric of things had to be cut, but the method is cheap and melodramatic.

A note on the unlikely

(1) The dialogue is often unlikely. Mrs Charmond tells Grace how hard it will be to give up Fitzpiers, to which the sanctimonious Grace replies: 'O, do struggle against it, and you will conquer!' Such a line belongs in a Victorian farce or melodrama. A wife is not commonly given to such a sentiment when talking to her husband's lover. Mrs Charmond whispers a few words in Grace's ear, then weeps. 'O my great God! . . . He's had you! Can it be – can it be!' cries Grace. The expression is silly in its attempt to strike a dramatic pose; its failure means melodrama and absurdity (Chapter 33).

(2) Situations are often uncommon: (*a*) Grace and Mrs Charmond spend the night in one another's arms in the woods; (*b*) a man-trap brings about a reconciliation; (*c*) a girl sells her beautiful hair; (*d*) a lover exposes himself to a storm to preserve the reputation of a beloved; (*e*) a man in bed dies of shock because a tree is felled; (*f*) a drop of rum makes a doctor drunk. Hardy's point, of course, is that uncommon events such as these make a good story. After all, there are more uncommon events reported in a daily newspaper than you will find in any novel by Hardy. The uncommonness is not in the characters. They are convincing.

The ending

Grace reassures her father that her reunion with Fitzpiers is for the best. What kind of future does she have? Ashamed of himself, he begs her forgiveness and asks her for a little love. Grace is prepared to take her time, until the man-trap determines the issue for her. Are we to assume that Fitzpiers is a changed man and that they will live happily ever after? Giles is dead and Marty heartbroken. Do Grace and Fitzpiers deserve more than them? Has the development of the novel been pointing towards their hard-earned happiness at the end? Does Hardy make it clear in *The Woodlanders* whether they are to be happy or not?

No. That is the answer to these questions. The following reasons may be adduced:

(1) The tone of the novel throughout has been lugubrious or mournful. Everything in the book, from that reference to Sophocles in Chapter 1 to the mourning Marty at the end, points to and contributes to a wretched ending.

(2) Fitzpiers, who once said that he could love several people at the same time, cannot change. He inhabits his own mind, his own imagination, his own Idea of love and women. If he is not in love with the idea of love, as is Eustacia Vye in Hardy's *The Return of the Native*, he is certainly in love with himself. No woman could be happy with him.

(3) Grace, who like Clym Yeobright in *The Return of the Native* was born to suffer the torments of a division within herself, cannot find a solution or happiness by marrying Fitzpiers. She needs a man who combines the homely virtues of Giles and the culture of Fitzpiers. But above all she needs peace within herself. In Chapter 40, Hardy describes her as 'an impressionable creature, who combined modern nerves with primitive feelings, and was doomed by such co-existence to be numbered among the distressed, and to take her scourgings to their exquisite extremity'. That seems clear enough.

(4) Percomb reappears at the end to remind us that three years have passed and to tell us that Little Hintock is 'a one-eyed place' full of bats and owls. It is a melancholy place.

(5) Melbury considers the reunion a forlorn hope since 'the woman walks and laughs somewhere at this very moment whose neck he'll be coling next year as he does hers tonight; and as he did Felice Charmond's last year; and Suke Damson's the year before . . .'.

(6) There is further evidence in Hardy's own writings.* He says in a letter to John Addington Symonds of 14 April 1889: 'I half promised

*Richard Little Purdy and Michael Millgate (editors), *The Collected Letters of Thomas Hardy*, Clarendon Press, Oxford, 1978.

to send you a copy of *The Woodlanders*. It is rather a failure towards the end.' What he means is explained in a letter of 19 July 1889 to Grein and Jarvis who were making a play out of *The Woodlanders*:

> You have probably observed that the ending of the story, as hinted rather than stated, is that the heroine is doomed to an unhappy life with an inconstant husband. I could not accent this strongly in the book; by reason of the conventions of the libraries etc. Since the story was written however truth to life is not considered quite such a crime in literature as it was formerly: and it is therefore a question for you whether you will accent this ending; or prefer to obscure it.

Hardy's intention, then, is clear. In another letter to W. Moy Thomas, of 7 August 1889, he wrote:

> In the story the reunited husband and wife are supposed to live ever after *un*happily! – or at any rate not quite happily . . .

Part 4

Hints for study

EXAMINATION QUESTIONS ON *The Woodlanders* should be designed to test your knowledge and understanding of the novel. In any novel worth reading there are passages that are guides to the theme; there are passages that describe or develop character; there are passages that are turning-points; there are passages that are dramatic highlights; there are incidents or episodes that express conflict; there are deliberate contrasts between scenes or characters; there is dialogue to throw light on character and develop plot and theme; and there is setting that reflects the tone and mirrors the theme of the novel as a whole.

What do you think merits close study in *The Woodlanders*? What are you going to remember most about the book in a few years' time and why? What are the novel's qualities, highlights or characteristics? Which passages or incidents should you study closely?

Setting and tone

(1) 'It was one of those sequestered spots outside the gates of the world where may usually be found more meditation than action, and more listlessness than meditation; where reasoning proceeds on narrow premises, and results in inferences wildly imaginative; yet where, from time to time, dramas of a grandeur and unity truly Sophoclean are enacted in the real, by virtue of the concentrated passions and closely-knit interdependence of the lives therein.' (Chapter 1)

Hardy sets the story in Hintock and states his intention. Does he achieve his intention? Is *The Woodlanders* tragedy or not? Do the characters have a universal appeal? Do they have tragic stature?

(2) 'There was now a distinct manifestation of morning in the air, and presently the bleared white visage of a sunless winter day emerged like a dead-born child.' (Chapter 4)

The Woodlanders is like an elegy, a song of mourning. Show how language and imagery create a feeling of melancholy.

(3) 'Here, as everywhere, the Unfulfilled Intention, which makes life what it is, was as obvious as it could be among the depraved crowds of a city slum. The leaf was deformed, the curve was crippled, the taper was interrupted; the lichen ate the vigour of the stalk, and the ivy slowly strangled to death the promising sapling.' (Chapter 7)

This is a central or key passage. Why?

(4) 'Next were more trees close together, wrestling for existence, their branches disfigured with wounds resulting from their mutual rubbings and blows.' (Chapter 42)

How is this passage related to ideas or themes in the novel?

The character of Marty South

What kind of person is she? What is her function in the story?

(1) See Chapter 2.

(2) 'The night in all its fulness met her flatly on the threshold, like the very brink of an absolute void, or the ante-mundane Ginnung-Gap believed in by her Teuton forefathers. For her eyes were fresh from the blaze, and here there was no street lamp or lantern to form a kindly transition between the inner glare and the outer dark. A lingering wind brought to her ear the creaking sound of two over-crowded branches in the neighbouring wood, which were rubbing each other into wounds . . .' (Chapter 3)

Marty is destined to suffer. She is a helpless creature.

(3) Giles and Marty are small figures in a vast landscape where 'their lonely courses formed no detached design at all, but were part of the pattern in the great web of human doings then weaving in both hemispheres from the White Sea to Cape Horn'. (Chapter 3)

(4) See the planting sequence in Chapter 8.

(5) 'Marty South alone, of all the women in Hintock and the world, had approximated to Winterborne's level of intelligent intercourse with Nature . . . They had been possessed of its finer mysteries as of commonplace knowledge; had been able to read its hieroglyphs as ordinary writing; to them the sights and sounds of night, winter, wind, storm, amid those dense boughs, which had to Grace a touch of the uncanny, and even of the supernatural, were simple occurrences whose origin, continuance, and laws they foreknew.' (Chapter 44)

Examine closely the whole passage. Show how, in the novel, Marty and Giles are at one with Nature. Demonstrate that they are part of one another. Grace is not at one with her surroundings. Why? Why does Hardy draw a contrast here between Grace and the other two? Show that this passage expresses a main idea in *The Woodlanders*. For example, it may remind you that Fitzpiers and Mrs Charmond hate their surroundings; the woodlanders accept their surroundings and life as it is. What is Hardy's point?

(6) Does Hardy idealise her? Is she a sentimental creation? See the last two paragraphs of Chapter 48.

The conflict in Grace Melbury

Fitzpiers or Giles?

(1) See the contrast between her gentility and Giles's rusticity. (Chapter 5)
(2) Giles considers himself a peasant in the light of her sophistication. (Chapter 9)
(3) 'They shouldn't have schooled her so monstrous high . . .' (Chapter 10)
(4) 'In truth, her ante-nuptial regard for Fitzpiers had been rather of the quality of awe towards a superior being than of tender solicitude for a lover. It had been based upon mystery and strangeness – the mystery of his past, of his knowledge, of his professional skill, of his beliefs. When this structure of ideals was demolished by the intimacy of common life, and she found him as merely human as the Hintock people themselves, a new foundation was in demand for an enduring and staunch affection . . .' (Chapter 28)

Fitzpiers had been unable to establish a union based on trust and confidence. For that reason, she is not particularly distressed to suspect his unfaithfulness. Chapter 28 presents a dramatic contrast between the way she sees Fitzpiers and the way she sees 'Autumn's brother'.

(5) As Grace and Giles talk about divorce laws, the omniscient narrator intrudes: 'They remained in thought, like children in the presence of the incomprehensible.' (Chapter 38)
(6) From the heart she says to Giles: 'You know what I feel for you – what I have felt for no other living man, what I shall never feel for a man again.' But a marriage vow dictates her behaviour.

The woodlanders

See Chapters 4, 6, 10, 20, 24, 25, 48. What is their function in the novel?

(1) The rustics are part of Hintock, they belong there. The woods provide them with a living.
(2) We are conscious of them in the background as part of the order of things.
(3) They provide a marked contrast with characters like Grace, Fitzpiers, and Mrs Charmond.
(4) They eat, work, play, and live without thinking about it. What is meant to be is meant to be. It is not their business to try and change anything.

(5) They have a sense of humour, a natural vitality, and an originality of expression.
(6) They talk common sense and they are also superstitious.
(7) They reflect the history, customs, and beliefs of an ancient Wessex.
(8) Hardy uses them to introduce and talk about main characters.
(9) They are often the voice of truth. In the voice there is often an ominous note, a warning.
(10) They comment on the action of the novel. Hardy does not idealise them but presents them as they are. The dialogue is refreshing, convincing, and, at times, difficult. A most helpful reference book is *The English Dialect Dictionary*, edited by Joseph Wright, Oxford University Press, 1970.

Examination questions

General advice

(1) Read the question carefully.
(2) Answer the question directly. Do not have a prepared answer.
(3) If there are two or three parts to the question, spend as much time on each in your answer unless you can show that one part is more important than the others. Sometimes a question will indicate how much time to spend on each part.
(4) From the novel select material that you can use to answer the question.
(5) List the main points you wish to make in the plan for the answer and support each one with reference to or quotation from the material you have selected.
(6) Make the conclusion a direct answer to the question.
(7) Read your answer carefully. Check everything. Remember that a quotation must make sense on its own.

Specimen questions and answers

(1) What do you think is the most dramatic scene in *The Woodlanders* and why?

The most dramatic scene in the novel ends with the death of Giles Winterborne. Ill, tired, and taking strength from the knowledge that he is the 'one man on earth in whom she believed absolutely', Giles withdraws to a primitive shelter that the rain penetrates. Grace puts Giles's hut in order and watches the small creatures of the woods 'who knew neither law nor sin'. They help to distract her. As part of the natural order of things they form a contrast with the plight of Giles and

Grace who remain apart for the sake of propriety and because of marriage vows. The rain pours down.

A storm comes. The night is violent. Grace feels entirely alone as the storm rages around the hut. It is as though 'an invisible colourless thing, was trampling and climbing over the roof making branches creak, springing out of the trees upon the chimney, popping its head into the flue, and shrieking and blaspheming at every corner of the walls.' The storm is an evil force, a spectre, without mercy. Nature is cruel. The devilish storm reflects and intensifies the tempest in Grace's heart. 'Sometimes a bough from an adjoining tree was swayed so low as to smite the roof in the manner of a gigantic hand smiting the mouth of an adversary, to be followed by a trickle of rain, as blood from the wound.' The violence and suffering created by this image remind us of the wounds that people and trees have been inflicting on one another throughout the novel. The image and the scene as a whole dramatise the theme of *The Woodlanders*.

People hurt one another and suffer. The thought of Giles outside makes Grace desperate, especially as she starts to recall that his face is thinner, his voice weak, and his walk feeble. Autumn's brother is near the dead of winter. It is a question of life or death. Grace realises that what matters is not what people will say or think. What matters is their love for one another. In the intense darkness, as the trees brandish their arms and the rain pours on, she calls out to Giles to come in. 'Come to me, dearest! I don't mind what they say or what they think of us any more.' Giles declines out of a sense of honour. Perhaps it is also because of that negative quality in him that makes him feel he is born to suffer.

In the morning the weather has cleared. A thrush comes to eat from the plate left out for Giles and a newt comes out to sun itself. Grace looks out on 'brown leaves', 'a black slug', 'dead boughs', and 'perishing woodbine stems'. The imagery is of disease and death. Fungi abound. 'Next were more trees close together, wrestling for existence, their branches disfigured with wounds resulting from their mutual rubbings and blows.' The anguish and torture felt by Grace are self-inflicted too. Rotting stumps rise from the moss 'like black teeth from green gums'. The image, like the situation of Giles, is grotesque. Hardy, the poet, is at work in this scene.

As evening comes on, the rain resumes, a cough reaches her ears. She who had been afraid to go to him in case they were discovered, now knows that propriety is killing her lover. Grace brings him delirious and dying back to the hut. He cannot recognise her. The scene is pathetic and dramatic because of the futility of Giles's self-sacrifice and because of Grace's realisation of his worth. They are both helpless figures. 'The purity of his nature, his freedom from the grosser passions, his scrupulous delicacy, had never been fully understood by Grace till this strange sacrifice in lonely juxtaposition to her own person was revealed'.

This scene is the climax of *The Woodlanders*. It is tense, urgent, and the narrative is fast-moving. Hardy has time for only one allusion. Chapters 41 and 42 form the climax as the central conflict in Grace and in the novel resolves itself in death and an irretrievable loss. Grace has lost that part of her she needed most and now has to reconcile herself to living with that part represented by Fitzpiers. Even Nature seems to feel the blow. 'Winterborne was gone, and the copses seemed to show the want of him; those young trees, so many of which he had planted, and of which he had spoken so truly when he said that he should fall before they fell, were at that very moment sending out their roots in the direction that he had given them with his subtle hand.'

---

(2) 'Fate, it seemed, would have it this way, and there was nothing to do but to acquiesce.' (Grace)

'Such miserable creatures of circumstance are we all!' (Fitzpiers)

Do characters in *The Woodlanders* control their own destinies or not? Argue a case.

The atmosphere of *The Woodlanders* is gloomy. There is a sense of fatality. 'The whole wood seemed to be a house of death... ' Melancholy is the keynote of the novel. There is a feeling that characters are doomed to unhappiness. The country around Hintock is no rustic retreat. Life is hard and the woodlanders know it.

This, however, does not mean that there is a Fate controlling the destinies of the characters. Marty South, for example, decides of her own accord to cut off her hair because she thinks Giles Winterborne is to marry Grace Melbury. She takes no positive action to try to win Giles. Instead she succumbs to what she thinks will happen and commits an act of self-sacrifice. She chooses to do so. Her attitude is negative and helpless, however devoted she may be to Giles. Of about twenty years of age, she behaves rather like an old woman. Throughout the novel she is a solitary, suffering figure.

Like Marty, Giles suffers and is alone. Engaged to and in love with Grace, he loses her to Fitzpiers. It is true that her father influences her choice with his social pretensions and it is true that Grace is intoxicated by the 'mystery and strangeness' of Fitzpiers. There is more to it, though. In Chapter 13, as he prunes the tree, Grace – below – indicates by her silence that she wishes to break their engagement. Instead of coming down the tree to talk to her, he climbs higher into the tree 'cutting himself off more and more from all intercourse with the sublunary world'. Surrounded by mist, he is a speck in the sky. It is an act of withdrawal if not self-destruction.

Grace returns to be frank with him. She wants them to be friends. She does not want an engagement. His reaction is extraordinary because it is so tired and resigned. Giles has nothing to say and he says it with a feeble voice. He remains in thought, shut off by the mist and the night. It is a symbolic scene in *The Woodlanders*. And in case we miss the significance of the scene, Hardy intrudes. 'If it be true as women themselves have declared, that one of their sex is never so much inclined to throw in her lot with a man for good and all as five minutes after she has told him such a thing cannot be, the probabilities are that something might have been done by the appearance of Winterborne on the ground beside Grace.' It is not just that Giles misses his opportunity; it is that he shuts himself off in a gloomy Niflheim, just as Marty proceeds into an utter void in Chapter 3. Later when there is the possibility of a divorce, Giles is hopeful but will not make a move. 'He would even repulse her – as a tribute to conscience.' Giles Winterborne determines his own fate.

Fitzpiers and Mrs Charmond create an illusion in their own imaginations and fall in love with it. Fitzpiers marries Grace because he thinks he loves her, but what he really loves is the image of her he has created to suit an idea in his head; he has an affair with Felice Charmond because she is like him and because his imagination makes much of a brief meeting with her in his student days. The fate of Fitzpiers, then, is determined by the kind of man he is; Mrs Charmond is less fortunate.

In Grace Melbury there is the naturalness of the woodlanders and the refinement of an education. She is torn between the two – between the world of Fitzpiers and Mrs Charmond and the world of Marty and Giles. There is also pressure from her father. But it is up to Grace to make the decision. She needs what both men represent and she cannot have both. Near the end, when she knows how much she loves Giles, she cannot breach the laws of marriage and social propriety. Finally she has to live with a compromise, a second best. That was the result of her own choice.

It is not therefore a question of acquiescence. Nobody in *The Woodlanders* is a wretched creature of circumstance. The major characters all have free will. They determine their own fates.

That is one line of argument. You may choose another.

---

(3) Show how Hardy contrasts the characters of Giles and Fitzpiers in order to highlight the conflict in Grace Melbury's mind.

The answer should be a character sketch of each and a clear statement about the conflict in Grace. Emphasise the differences between the men.

Giles: Chapters 3, 8, 9, 28, 39, 41.

Fitzpiers: Chapters 14, 17, 19, 25, 28, 35.

(4) Hardy said that *The Woodlanders* was his favourite story. What do you think of it?

The answer should be a critical review of the novel in which you may discuss theme, setting, characterisation, structure, language. Your job is to highlight what you think are the strengths and weaknesses of the novel as a whole. You may adopt whatever point of view you wish, provided your claims are supported with evidence from the novel in the form of reference or quotation. The answer need not be as general as the question.

(5) 'Melbury is not the only person in *The Woodlanders* who lacks judgment.' Discuss.

> (*i*) List the blunders made by Grace's father and see Chapters 31 and 32.
> (*ii*) Show how Grace's judgment is confused.
> (*iii*) Show how Fitzpiers and Mrs Charmond create their own fantasies.
> (*iv*) Where does Giles Winterborne stand? If his judgment is sound what does he lack?
> (*v*) Did Marty have to cut her hair off?

A REMINDER:
What the examiner wants most of all is your response to what you have read. Say what you think.

Part 5

Suggestions for further reading

The text

The recommended text is:
Thomas Hardy's *The Woodlanders*, The New Wessex Edition, Macmillan, London, 1974.

Biography

GITTINGS, ROBERT: *Young Thomas Hardy*, Heinemann, London, 1975.
GITTINGS, ROBERT: *Thomas Hardy's Later Years*, Little, Brown, New York, 1978.
OREL, HAROLD: *The Final Years of Thomas Hardy, 1912–1928*, University Press of Kansas, Lawrence, Manhattan, Wichita, 1976.

Background

WILLIAMS, MERRYN: *Thomas Hardy and Rural England*, Macmillan, London, 1972.

Criticism

GREGOR, IAN: *The Great Web*, Faber, London, 1974.
KRAMER, DALE: *The Forms of Tragedy*, Macmillan, London, 1975.
PINION, F. B.: *Thomas Hardy: Art and Thought*, Rowman and Littlefield, Totowa, New Jersey, 1977.
STEWART, J. I. M.: *Thomas Hardy: A Critical Biography*, Longman, London, 1971.
THURLEY, GEOFFREY: *The Psychology of Hardy's Novels*, University of Queensland Press, St. Lucia, Queensland, 1975.
VIGAR, PENELOPE: *The Novels of Thomas Hardy*, Athlone Press, London, 1974.

The most useful books for insights into *The Woodlanders* are by Gregor, Pinion, and Stewart.

The author of these notes

STEWART LUKE was born in Stirling, Scotland in 1936 and educated in schools in Dundee and Arbroath. After his family moved to Australia in 1952, he read Honours in English at the University of Adelaide. He taught English literature and languages in secondary schools. For ten years he was Senior Lecturer in English at Torrens College of Advanced Education, Adelaide. He now holds a similar position at the Adelaide College of the Arts and Education. He has published book reviews and various literary articles, and is also the author of the *York Notes* volume on Hardy's *The Return of the Native.*